The Man Who Loved Wasps

Books by HOWARD ENSIGN EVANS

A Naturalist's Years in the Rocky Mountains

The Natural History of the Long Expedition to the Rocky Mountains, 1819–1820

Pioneer Naturalists:
The Description and Naming of North American Plants and Animals

Cache la Poudre: The Natural History of a Rocky Mountain River
(with Mary Alice Evans, junior author)

The Natural History and Behavior of North American Beewolves
(with K. M. O'Neill, junior author)

The Pleasures of Entomology: Portraits of Insects and the People Who Study Them

Insect Biology: A Textbook of Entomology

Australia: A Natural History (with Mary Alice Evans, junior author)

The Biology of Social Insects
(coedited with M. D. Breed and C. D. Michener)

William Morton Wheeler, Biologist (with Mary Alice Evans, senior author)

The Wasps (with Mary Jane West Eberhard, junior author)

Life on a Little-Known Planet

The Comparative Ethology and Evolution of Sand Wasps

Wasp Farm

Studies on the Comparative Ethology of Digger Wasps of the Genus Bembix

The Man Who Loved Wasps

A Howard Ensign Evans Reader

Edited and with an Introduction
by Mary Alice Evans

Foreword by Edward O. Wilson

JOHNSON BOOKS
AN IMPRINT OF BOWER HOUSE
DENVER

Cover Illustration and Design by Margaret McCullough
Internal Layout by Debra B. Topping and Eric Christensen

Library of Congress Cataloging-in-Publication Data
Evans, Howard Ensign.
    The man who loved wasps: a Howard Ensign Evans reader / Howard Ensign Evans; edited and with an Introduciton by Mary Alice Evans.
        p. cm.
    Incudes index.
ISBN 978-1-55566-350-6
    1. Natural history. 2. Insects. I. Enan s, Mary Alice. II. Title.
    QH45.2.E93 2005

2004020312

10 9 8 7 6 5 4 3 2

Contents

Contents

Foreword

by Edward O. Wilson

HOWARD ENSIGN EVANS was a quiet man, careful in his choice of spoken words to the point of taciturnity, yet immensely articulate. In conversation he usually maintained a neutral expression—I hesitate to say poker faced—but inwardly he was a deeply emotional, caring person, whose soul, as these essays show, opened outward with a poet's grace in the presence of the natural world.

Professionally, he was an entomologist of the first rank. Among other accomplishments, he was arguably the world's leading authority on wasps. That might seem strange to those of different background, even those who love nature. The little creatures that engrossed him are so different from mammals, birds, and other familiar large animals that they might have come from some other planet. Viewed up close, however, beyond the vision of the vast majority of people who attend to insects with little more than mosquito nets and bug spray, exists a world of profound complexity and startling beauty.

That world is also to be valued as part of the biosphere on which human life depends. Insects rule the biodiversity of Earth. Their 900,000 known species outnumber those of all other organisms combined (although bacteria are destined to overtake them soon, when diagnostic methods improve a bit more). The actual number of insect species, comprising both those given a scientific name and those yet to be discovered, is probably somewhere between two and ten times larger. Such is the circumstance that prompted Evans, in one of his better turned phrases, to describe Earth as a little-known planet.

The number of insects belonging to all these species and alive at any given moment has been estimated (by the British ecologist C. B. Williams) to be about a million trillion. In biomass they exceed all other animals. The ants alone weigh approximately as much as all the humans.

It should come as no surprise therefore that insects are the chief pollinators, predators, scavengers, and earth-movers of the land environment. If all insects suddenly disappeared, most of the terrestrial ecosystems would collapse, and with them all but a few populations of human survivors. Humanity would become a critically endangered species. Sad to say, we need insects but they don't need us.

Thus, in giving a public voice to insects and other small creatures, melded so richly from a lifetime of expertise and aesthetic feeling, Howard Evans is explaining something important. He is telling us that just because a handful of insect species compete with us for food and carry some of our diseases and otherwise annoy us, we should not let harm fall to the vast majority that run Earth's ecological machinery.

In this essay collection Howard Evans has other things to say about the living world and ourselves. In plain yet evocative language, he makes clear that the world is an eternal frontier, and in search of microwildernesses you will find your back yard also to be a frontier. Having taken billions of years to evolve, the living world will never run out of mystery, novelty, and excitement—providing we don't thuggishly destroy it. Conserving as much as possible of life on the little-known planet is the priceless heritage Evans would have us bestow on future generations.

Preface

THE SONGS OF BIRDS, the hum of insects, the fragrance of meadows freshly washed after a summer storm—these are among the many rewards for persons attuned to the natural world. As the earth's only sapient beings, we should be keen to learn the meanings of nature's sights and sounds—meanings that render them even more precious. But we must quickly be out and about, for our days slip by one by one, and one by one species are fleeing to beyond the limits of our sprawl, some to their doom.

As a farm boy in the Connecticut valley, I grew up to bird-song and the chirping of crickets, to flower-filled meadows and to woodlands where pink lady's slipper orchids grew. Those meadows and woodlands are long since gone, and I have fled west, where hope is still sometimes possible. The essays in this collection were written over a third of a century and reflect diverse aspects of my career as a teacher and researcher. I do not apologize that they are biased toward insects, which are, after all, the most abundant of terrestrial animals, though little appreciated by most people. My parents were chagrined that I became an entomologist; but it has proved a life filled with wonders and with opportunities. It seemed to me, early on, that students of nature should try to convey to others some of the excitement of their field, and in so doing try to persuade people to restrain their needs for luxuries and thrills, as well as their ability to add immoderately to a human population that already challenges the earth's carrying capacity—in deference to an already sorely stressed natural world.

I was lucky to find, more than forty years ago, a companion who was not only tolerant of my perversities but as eager as I to revel in nature's largesse and to inquire into its workings. Mary Alice and I have coauthored three books and she is coauthor of three essays included here, as acknowledged.

Howard E. Evans
Fort Collins, Colorado

Introduction

My Memories of
Howard Ensign Evans

Mary Alice Evans

WARD AND I WERE MARRIED in the spring of 1954. To tell of our many years together could fill a book or two or more, so in this introduction I can only give a glimpse of what was a long and happy life together. Howard was a quiet man, not given to idle conversation, a scholar with a penchant for insects (especially wasps), a hard worker, and a talented writer. He was the kindest man I ever knew, but he also did not hesitate to protest anything he did not like or of which he did not approve, such as poorly written books or papers (especially on biological subjects), shoddy workmanship, or politics and politicians who had no respect for the environment. He liked classical music, collected records, tapes, and CDs, and enjoyed attending concerts. If a musician played a wrong note in a piece, he heard it. His keen hearing gave him a distinct advantage when we went on bird walks, as he could recognize and identify each bird by its song, whereas I had to see it to recognize it. The first word our oldest daughter learned to say was "bird" because her father took her along on his bird walks when I was housebound with our second baby.

We spent the first six years of our marriage in Ithaca, New York (my hometown), when Howard was on the Cornell University faculty. We owned a small house on eight acres on a hill south of town. Below us Cayuga Lake stretched to the north, the university with its towers was visible to our right on East Hill, and West Hill loomed to our left up the west side of the lake. All three of our children were born there. The land also supported many insects as well as a large garden, which we shared with my parents and the insects. *Wasp Farm*, Howard's first popular book, describes our life there, and sometimes away from there.

In 1959 Howard took his first sabbatical leave from Cornell's Entomology Department, and we spent most of the year in Mexico. We rented a house in Cuernavaca, southwest of Mexico City, and while we were there we employed a maid who was unique in many ways. She was probably about eighteen, illiterate, loved the children, and also apparently enjoyed catching insects. She would dash into the house, grab a bug net, and catch wasps and butterflies in the backyard. Howard remarked at the time that we probably never again would have a maid, especially one like that, and he was right. When Howard looked back on that trip he wondered how we ever had the courage to go with three preschool children in a second-hand car to a foreign country.

When Howard transferred from Cornell to the Museum of Comparative Zoology at Harvard University, we went from a rather rural area in upstate New York to the suburbs of Boston. We moved to Lexington, rather than Cambridge, because the schools there had a reputation for being among the best in the nation, and our three children were almost of school age. While living there we took many summer field trips, several of which were to the Jackson Hole Biological Station in Moran, Wyoming. Our summers there enabled Howard to work on wasp behavior in two national parks—Grand Teton and Yellowstone. It was also there that we started to teach our children backpacking by first having them carry their sleeping bags, and then, as they grew, more and more of the family's camping equipment. We loved those regal mountains, their twisting trails, wildflowers up to our elbows, glaciers, moose and bears now and then, and all that goes with mountain wilderness.

We usually stayed at the station for at least six weeks and then started home in time for school by way of the Great Sand Dunes National Monument in southern Colorado. That was sand wasp paradise, and also heaven for anyone interested in studying sand wasp behavior. Later, when we were permanently living in Colorado, Howard and his students spent many summers there, as we did as a family, too.

While at Harvard, Howard did not do much teaching, so he had a lot more time for research and writing. Scientific papers flew out, especially after his busy summers as well as his South American and Australian trips. His popular books included *Life on a Little-Known Planet*, which probably brought him the most fame. The book was translated into several languages, and even landed him a spot on television's *Today Show*. "Back," he used to say, "when television amounted to something!" Another popular book, which we had both worked on, was a biography of Harvard's "Ant Man," Professor William Morton Wheeler. Dr. Wheeler's daughter lived in the family home on Beacon Hill, had kept all her father's papers, and allowed me to go through them and take notes. She also gave me lunch when I was there and answered any questions I might have. After several years of working there, I even helped her walk her five black Scotties around the streets.

Another extended trip was to Australia in 1969 and 1970. We took the children and enrolled them in the local schools in Canberra, the capital. We found the schools quite different from those back home. The school year was "upside-down," so when we arrived in August it was the beginning of the third session, with the summer vacation starting in December. Also, boys' and girls' schools were separate. Howard and I noticed, when we helped with homework, that the Australian schools were more like those we had attended when we were young than our children's Lexington schools. Howard and I went back to Australia several times after that (without our children), not only for Howard's wasp studies but also to collect material for a book on Australia's unique natural history, which the Smithsonian Institution published.

Near the end of Howard's tenure at Harvard and as our children were approaching college age, we began to think about moving farther out into the western suburbs of Boston to escape the ever-increasing traffic, development, and general hassle of city life. Harvard had acquired an old missile site in Bedford just west of Lexington and planned to improve it as a field station. Howard liked it there, where he wouldn't have to face Cambridge congestion. We found a house near the site that we liked, but our bid on it was turned down. This brought on thoughts of moving further west, so we studied a map of the country and picked out some places we thought we might like to live. Then we inquired at nearby colleges and universities about possible openings. Colorado State University (CSU) was the first to respond. With the approval of our children, we then moved to Fort Collins, Colorado, in the summer of 1973. The Entomology and Zoology Departments had just been combined in a new building, and as Howard considered his research basic science, he was pleased to become a part of the department. Our family was thrilled with the spectacular scenery and easy access to high-country hiking trails and wondered why we hadn't migrated to the West earlier.

Howard taught several different courses at CSU from 1973 until his retirement in 1983. During those years he had some excellent and enthusiastic graduate students. Although at Harvard, Cornell, and Kansas State (where he had been before we met) he had had fine doctoral candidates and post-doctoral students, at CSU he had more time to work in the field with each one. Further, he was in charge of the insect collection, a very important tool for all entomologists. In the collection, one of the poorest groups represented was the Odonata, the dragonflies and damselflies, because pests had destroyed most of the specimens before he arrived. So Howard said let's start over and build up that part of the collection. He "appointed" me curator of Odonata, and we spent the next several years touring around the state collecting in or near any wet spot we could find. Our exploration of Colorado was such fun that we decided to do the same in New Mexico. It had become obvious to us that little was known at that time about Odonata in the Rocky Mountain West. And, of course, as we traveled, we also continued watching and collecting digger wasps.

Over the years Howard received several honors, the highest being elected to the National Academy of Sciences. In his lifetime he published more than 260 scientific papers, wrote more than sixty articles for popular magazines and papers, and produced sixteen books, some strictly scientific and some popular. He loved his work, and consequently he never took any administrative position that would not allow him time to continue his wasp behavior studies, and he always took his sabbatical leaves to do research in the field. Retirement for him meant finally being able to skip department meetings and other institutional duties. One of the first things we did was move out of town and into the mountains at 7,800 feet. As soon as we had done that, we started to write a natural history of our favorite local river, the Cache la Poudre. We had hiked its length and most of the tributaries with our children, noting the rocks, trees, birds, flowers, insects, and so on. Then we searched for books and papers that would tell us more of its history. We spent five years in the final book preparation, enjoying every minute of it. Of course, while we were so engaged, Howard was also thinking about other books and articles he might write now that he had the quiet place and time to do so.

Howard's last book, *A Naturalist's Years in the Rocky Mountains*, was about our years of living in the mountains and the plants and animals that shared our time there. We spent a delightful thirteen years observing all that went on around us, and then we began to realize that we were getting older and slower. It was becoming more difficult to do what we needed to do (such as chopping wood and shoveling snow) to live in the mountains year round.

We were fortunate to find an apartment in Fort Collins near one of the city parks, where Howard could take his bug net and check out the insect fauna on nice days. He also spent time on campus with the insect collection, putting names on the wasps that needed them. And he would bring me the dragonflies and damselflies as they accumulated. I could no longer see well enough to catch any, or maybe my swinging arm was too slow, but I could still name specimens caught by others. We did take one last trip abroad to Brazil, mostly to see the Amazon, but we went as tourists rather than researchers.

Howard died suddenly on July 18, 2002, and I knew that was as he would have wished. Although I was saddened, I was pleased to have shared almost fifty years of his life.

1

Discovering Life on Earth

This essay was written soon after I had moved west and begun to explore (with my family) some of Colorado's wonderful mountain country. It was published in Sierra Club Bulletin *(now* Sierra) *in January 1977. I have omitted a sentence or two.*

WE LIVE AT THE THRESHOLD of the Space Age. The Industrial Revolution is not much more than a hundred years old, yet our technology has made such giant leaps that we have been able to sit in our living rooms and watch men walk on the moon. But already that is an old story; more recently we have seen the surface of Mars in living color. It is a red planet after all, but devoid of Martians and so far as we can be sure, of any living things. We have seen something of the surface of Venus, and of Mercury and Jupiter. Futurists and science-fiction writers will have to move farther out in space; the planets and their moons are desolate and rock strewn, forbiddingly cold or hellishly hot. Perhaps we may yet build habitable space stations or find planets where life exists or can be transplanted. So long as the earth has resources we may reasonably divert into space exploration, we will surely do so. Man is a searcher, a builder, a dreamer ... and a destroyer.

Yet these are exciting times. Who has not followed the accomplishments of the space program? A comfortable way to become a pioneer—by diverting some tax dollars and watching the results on TV. Rather different from our forefathers, who hacked through

1

virgin forests and traversed endless deserts to seek el Dorados they seldom found. The wilderness so forbidding to them is now largely strung with fences and highways, speckled with pizza parlors and automobile junkyards. Will space someday lose its incredible distances, the planets their desolation? I doubt it, but then I suspect that my grandfather doubted men would ever walk on the moon.

With the broadened perspective the space program has provided, perhaps each of us should design our own program, focused on the only planet that to most of us seems worth exploring. Is there life on earth? Yes, several million kinds, many of them a good deal more incredible than the creations of science-fiction writers. Are there clear waters, breezes rich with oxygen and the odors of the forest, meadows spangled with butterflies, nights adorned with fireflies and haunted by owls? All of these and much more. Do we take time to revel in the richness of our planet, to explore its inner workings, to add to an understanding of its complexities?

The equipment needed for an earthly space walk is minimal: suitable clothing, food, a sleeping bag for the more adventurous, perhaps a notebook and pencil, a camera, a pair of binoculars, but most of all, a keen eye and a soul that responds to a jagged cloud, a moss-covered boulder, the call of a raven. This is the earth! And I am an astronaut, walking on the best of planets, seeing things never seen before: sunlight filtered through an arrangement of branches; a cloud of midges dancing over a stream; a configuration of gulls wheeling in a sky meshed with cirrus; a giant ice crystal flanking a February stream. Time, space and I have never before had this conjunction, nor will we again.

Just a few months ago, my family and I explored a nearby canyon in the foothills of the Rockies. We had been there many times before, but it was good to visit again, with its particularly jocular stream, its rocky overhang where we first learned to recognize alum root, its giant Douglas firs still clinging to life despite a too-great intimacy with electric storms. But we had never been there on a warm and breezy October day, when the cottonwoods were so freely casting their gold leaves about, when Townsend's solitaires were so enthusiastically serenading the demise of summer. Here and there, in quiet stretches, the stream passed over stones that barely broke the surface film, producing little swirls that in the sunlight formed dark sequins margined with silver. A pygmy owl flew ahead of us carrying a mouse, seemingly happy enough to be about in midday, but perhaps not so happy to be mobbed by noisy chickadees. A late solitary wasp was dragging a paralyzed spider along a bank. Since wasp behavior is a specialty of mine, I took the liberty of capturing them—a new record, as it turned out.

The possibilities of earth exploration are vastly multiplied when we consider that there are several levels of discovery. First, the renewal of acquaintance with the familiar—familiar, yet in the flow of time never quite the same. Then, the finding of something that is personally novel—a species of bird observed for the first time (as the pygmy owl was for us), a snowcapped peak seen from the crest of a mountain trail, a gentian blooming among the weeds in one's back yard. Finally, the discovery of facts new to science—often little things, like my spider-hunting wasp, but sometimes essential pieces of bigger puzzles. The first two are available to everyone, the last to persons well prepared in some facet of natural science—but it doesn't take a Ph.D. to discover novel associations in the enormously complex tapestry of nature.

In fact, how well do we know the planet earth? Incredibly, we have only the roughest idea as to how many kinds of plants and animals the earth supports—estimates range from three million to fifteen million or more. Biologists agree that a high percentage of these are still unknown to science (more especially in the tropics). According to an estimate published in *Science* a few years ago, only fifteen percent of all organisms have been described. I question this, and would place the figure closer to fifty percent. That these estimates are at such variance demonstrates just how ignorant we are of life on earth!

To say that a plant or animal is "known to science" simply means that someone has described it and given it a name. Often we know next to nothing about its way of life. We have total knowledge of no living creature. Even the honeybee, well known to the ancients and still the subject of innumerable books and scientific treatises, is still being studied intensively. How often we discover too late the subtleties and complexities of nature, as when we transport a devastating pest to a new continent, or overthrow an aquatic ecosystem with our pollutants. Only after many years did we fathom the far-reaching effects of DDT, and only now are we closing some of our rivers to fishing because of the accumulation of PCBs. Should we be concerned over disturbances in the ozone layer? Should we worry that the "greenhouse effect" caused by increased airborne chemicals may someday melt the Antarctic ice cap and flood our coastal cities? How many people will the earth support, and how many and what animal and plant species do we dare eliminate without reducing our own viability as a species? How can we afford to be so ignorant of the planet that is our home?

To all of us the earth is a vast frontier we may enter here and there, casually or deeply, as we please. Unfortunately we often take it for granted—a place to dump the tailings of our civilization—or even become bored with it ("if you've seen one redwood, you've seen them all"). To know the earth does take some awareness, some sensitivity, some preparation. In a culture obsessed with comfort, it is doubtless simpler to look at the sterile Martian rocks on television than to become one's own astronaut, picking one's way across the incredible plains and forests of Earth.

Yes, there is life on earth, and for all we know, nowhere else. To be sure, untrammeled nature is becoming increasingly scarce, yet we are lucky to be born of this century, when wilderness, no longer a threat to be overcome, remains still with us, though in small measure; when we know so much, yet are so aware of our ignorance; when we have so many aids to probing the heart of nature. Technology need not be our undoing if we dedicate it to exploring the earth as a home for all earthlings. Even you and I may be astronauts and, however modest our capacities, may find landscapes not fully explored. At the very least we will find assurance that we live on a planet so incredibly rich and precious that its preservation must be a matter of highest priority.

2

On Waking to Bird Song

I put together these thoughts in 1975. I have since been to Australia again and this time did hear a lyrebird in the wild. I have never kept a "life list" of birds. I would rather hear a meadowlark a thousand times than list a thousand birds. This essay appeared in The Living Wilderness (*later* Wilderness).

THIS MORNING IT WAS A FLICKER. Out of a melange of dreams, of half-thoughts straddling the border of consciousness, suddenly all was in focus. How good to have another day, a flicker-announced day! From my bed I could visualize the flash of red in his wings; and remember the yellow-shafted flicker of my youth, and finding a nest in an ancient willow, full of noisy nestlings. Bold, resilient, shattering the dawn with a loud, clear call to action.

The other day it was a meadowlark, "our" meadowlark, with a voice just a bit different from others in the neighborhood. The West is meadowlarks, and with luck one can hear them any month of the year—though their song is never so sweet as in February, when one is hoping for spring but not finding much evidence of it. How good that meadowlarks and flickers still flourish in a world greatly altered by mankind. Why did the passenger pigeons vanish, when mourning doves nest in the black locusts not far from our back door?

When I was a boy I slept on a porch at the back of our New England farmhouse, a place of wonderful odors: new-mown hay,

7

lilacs, rich manure. Spring mornings I would wake to the Baltimore oriole that owned the elm tree in the back yard. I have never again heard an oriole with a song quite like that one, for oriole songs are as individualistic as the meadowlark's, perhaps more so. Strangely, I still remember that song in detail, just as (for no reason at all) I remember a particular limb on our nearest apple tree, a limb just right for swinging one's legs and tossing one's thoughts. I have never again met such an apple tree, or such an oriole.

I remember, too, waking in a sleeping bag one morning years ago on a hilltop in the Catskills. Out of the mists came a call as lean and elemental as the spruces themselves: the call of the white-throated sparrow. We had been trapping small mammals for somebody's research (not mine) and had run out of supplies. But our car had broken down, so we were living on rodent bait—peanut butter and oatmeal. White-throats will forever remind me of misty forests—and of peanut butter and oatmeal.

I am not sure which is more exciting, to hear for the first time a particularly renowned singer or the voice of an old friend after a long absence. For many years I had heard stories about the kookaburra, the famous "laughing jackass" of Australia. Then one morning, camped in the bush not far from Perth, I was treated to a raucous chorus of kookaburras—a sound more than worthy of that fascinating continent. Just a few mornings ago a loon called from Terry Lake, where we live, just against the eastern foothills of the Colorado Rockies. The last time I had heard a loon we were camped on Togue Ponds, at the foot of Mount Katahdin. As I drifted off to partial sleep again, I was again in Maine, picking blueberries and casting for trout. Both the kookaburra and the loon are said to "laugh," but these are laughs from other worlds than ours!

Speaking of strange bird songs, I remember my first field trip to Texas. We had been exploring caves for salamanders and beetles and had camped in a scrubby area far from any town. I woke to a cacophony so strange that I could not imagine what manner of beast was afoot. A series of hoarse "coos" descended the scale and was followed by a scramble of purrs and loud clacking noises—an alarm clock far more alarming than any invented by man. It was, of course, that most incredible and precious of birds, the roadrunner. Perhaps the most ethereal song I have heard is that of the mountain whistler (or rufous-throated solitaire) of the West Indies, a song so moving that, no matter how often one hears it, he must stop whatever he is doing and listen. For six weeks I participated in the Smithsonian Institution's biological survey of Dominica, and fortunately I could find many excuses for visiting the dripping forests where the whistler lives. But I must sadly confess that the song has gone completely from my memory, just as a profound poem is so much more difficult to remember than doggerel. How I would love to hear it again!

Bird songs need not be complex to be moving. The crested bellbird of Australia has a single note in his repertory—but how he uses it! I well remember waking among the mulgas of central Australia to its unique pattern of notes, rather like a letter of the Morse code being played over and over on an alto recorder. Monotonous and melancholy, yes, but perfectly suited to that dry and dreary landscape. And the bellbird is a marvelous ventriloquist, invariably found to be calling from a tree other than the one imagined.

Of course there are many wonderful songs I have never heard: the nightingale, for instance. A number of times in Australia I was in the habitat of the lyrebird, but evidently not at quite the right season, for I have heard the effervescence of that remarkable bird only on records. And only in books have I encountered the bou-bou shrike, one of a number of birds that perform antiphonal duets: that is, male and female sing together in alternating phrases, beautifully timed to produce a single, complex song.

I was amused to learn that Charles Hartshorne, in his book *Born to Sing*, has developed a rating scale for bird songs. Each species is rated 1 to 9 on six factors: loudness, complexity, tone, continuity, organization and imitativeness. Of North American birds, the hermit thrush is awarded the highest score (47 out of a possible 54). The western meadowlark is not far behind with 45. Among species outside the United States, the crested bellbird merits a 45, the mountain whistler 42. The poor old flicker is relegated to a chapter entitled "less well-equipped singers," as is the kookaburra.

I suppose there is something to be said for this, but I tend to rate bird songs more by the moods and memories they evoke. The red-winged blackbird doesn't sing at all, really, but what is more effective than his "o-ka-lee" in bringing to mind an April morning in a misty cattail marsh? More than once, alone in a strange city, I have been reassured by the call of that most mundane and unmusical of birds, the house sparrow. And bird song on waking–almost any song–is an aperitif and an affirmation: it may, after all, be worth getting up!

I have been intrigued by some of the manipulations of the ethologists. Song sparrows, for example, when foster-reared from the egg by canaries in a soundproof room, nevertheless produce their typical song when they reach maturity. But white-crowned sparrows are very different. When isolated as nestlings, they grow up to produce a song quite unlike their normal song. But if exposed as nestlings to a recording of the song of the adult, they are able to reproduce it perfectly when, many months later, they acquire the ability to sing. For reasons it is hard to understand, song sparrows inherit their song, but white-crowns must learn their song from their parents–but they must learn it long before they are able to practice it.

With sophisticated equipment, it is possible to do some exciting experiments with bird song. The indigo bunting, for example, produces a warble consisting mostly of notes in pairs: 11233445566. Stephen Emlen, of Cornell University, has cut and spliced his tapes so as to produce a song with all the same notes, but in a very different order, none of them paired: 12345613456.

This song, when played to a male defending a territory, produces a response indistinguishable from that of the usual song. But when spacing of the notes is increased or decreased (for example 1 1 2 3 3 4 4 5 5 6 6) there is little response to the song. Evidently only certain aspects of the song convey meaning to other members of the species. Perhaps this shouldn't surprise us. After all, if we humans said only what was meaningful, we probably wouldn't say very much.

We can't all be ethologists, much as we may admire their discoveries. Or poets—for bird song has inspired poets as different as Li T'ai-po and Keats, and composers as different as Handel and Respighi. One need only have a spirit that is tuned to the wind and the notes that float upon it. The meadowlark is singing! The news from the Middle East may be bad, but the news from the meadow reminds us that although the world is imperfect, renewal and rededication are possible.

3

From *Wasp Farm*

When we bought our first home, near Ithaca, N.Y. (for $11,000!), we converted our eight acres into Wasp Farm, and that became the title of my first non-technical book. It was published by The Natural History Press in 1963 and nominated for a National Book Award that year. It has been through three reprintings in paperback and as of this writing is still in print (Cornell University Press). One chapter appeared in Hal Borland's anthology of nature writing, Our Natural World *(1965). I include here only two short excerpts.*

Wasp Farm and How It Came to Be

Readers who expect to find in this book a sequel to George Orwell's *Animal Farm* will be disappointed; it is about wasps, not about humans disguised as wasps, nor, I trust, about wasps imbued with human characteristics. Yet perhaps there is something Orwellian about the inexorability of wasps' lives, the tyranny of their instincts. Wasps share our planet but live in a different world. All about us they wind out their little lives, unaware that man is lord and master of the earth.

Ours is a world of vast panoramas, a world of jet transport, of atomic energy, of dawning world government or of vast devastation. Of what use are wasps? None, really. And yet they might save us. This is what I mean: so long as man is intent upon populating every square inch of the world and upon wringing every last drop of sustenance out of the earth, he is doomed. Even if things go well, and each of our great-grandchildren is blessed

13

with a square yard of pavement, a roof, and all the comforts of twenty-first century living, what will have become of our heritage, of our ties with our origins? Will our great-grandchildren still read Thoreau?

> *I went to the woods because I wished to live deliberately, to*
> *front only the essential facts of life, and see if I could not*
> *learn what it had to teach ...*

What is man? As a predator he is unrivaled but not unique; the world is full of lesser predators. It is as artist and scientist that he is unique, the only being able, in considerable measure, to understand and appreciate the world of which he is a part. And that world is fast slipping away from him—the real world, that is—to be replaced by an artificial world, built of concrete, steel and chrome. Our eyes are upon the vastness of space, our dreams of other worlds, unexplored, unimaginable. Once again the thrill of the primeval, the challenge of unwarped nature! Yet our own tired planet still has its frontiers: my own back yard is full of them, full of creatures that put to shame the science-fiction writer's men of Mars. We would do well to spend less time reaching for the stars, to value some things above comfort and the expansion of our economy. We would do well, now and then, to stretch out on the good earth with a notebook, camera, or sketch pad and chronicle the lives of some of our less self-important neighbors.

It was thoughts such as these that impelled us, a few years ago, to buy the eight acres of woods, fields, and brambles which became Wasp Farm. It needn't have been wasps, of course: beetles would have done nearly as well, or tardigrades. Tardigrades: there is a frontier for you. Have you ever seen one? I may not know where to find the distributor in my car; I may stumble over the laws of thermodynamics; but I have seen a tardigrade! Several, in fact. But wasps are my specialty. I won't try to unravel the various plots and subplots that resulted in the channeling of my interests into wasps. Suffice it to say there is (or ought to be) a specialist on everything. And there's a good deal to be said for wasps, as you will see.

Finding a place to establish Wasp Farm was not easy. We were newlyweds, in fact not yet married when we started our search. We soon found that the size of a mortgage is strictly determined by the size of one's salary, and in affairs of this sort a teacher's salary doesn't amount to much. We found, naturally, that people who want to sell a house don't advertise its potentialities for wasps, and these have to be sniffed out while one is pretending to inspect the well. The place we finally selected had a house which soon proved too small for our rapidly growing family, but which overlooked a broad panorama of woods, meadows, and lake. Its eight acres were rocky and mostly covered with bushes and brambles (but a good many wasps nest in brambles, and wild blackberries are delicious eating). One corner of the land had a patch of woods, mostly weed trees like poplars and locusts, but sufficient to support plenty of birds and insects and several patches of bloodroot. I suppose the thing that attracted us most was the sand pit in one corner of the land, for many wasps require sandy soil for digging their nests. The sand was not of very high quality, but sand is a scarce commodity in parts of upstate New York, and digger wasps can't afford to be choosy.

I use the past tense because, alas, we have since sold our eight acres of hilltop and been lured to Suburbia. But Wasp Farm is, after all, more an attitude than any particular piece of land. I doubt if our place had any more wasps than many a place of comparable size. To the people we bought it from it had been a chicken farm. To the present occupants, who knows? The wasp inhabitants have once again slipped back into obscurity, and it is all the same to them. But wherever we happen to be, wasps are king. I would hesitate to call our tiny chunk of Suburbia a farm; it is rather a base of operations for summer travel and winter reflection. This has been a long winter and our first winter away from Wasp Farm. From it emerged this book, a personal and slightly nostalgic account of wasps we have known and admired.

Wasps are not nearly the formidable creatures most people believe. It is true that the females of most species sting. The sting is a modification of the egg-laying apparatus and thus is not present in the males. The sting functions primarily to paralyze the insects or spiders on which wasps prey, so that they can be stored in a fresh but immobile state for their larvae to eat. Secondarily it can be used in defense, but most wasps have to be handled pretty roughly before they will sting. I often spend whole summers working with wasps without being stung a single time. In the social wasps, such as the hornets, yellow jackets, and common paper wasps, the sting has lost its importance in paralyzing the prey and serves mainly in defense of the colony. The nests of these wasps often occur around the haunts of man, and he who manhandles them learns a bitter lesson. But the social wasps make up only a small portion of the total kinds of wasps. Most wasps live solitary, unobtrusive lives, and to be stung by one is about as likely and as serious as being struck by a falling acorn: though for a few moments it is distinctly more painful.

How to Attract Wasps, and Why

Some years ago I read a book by that delightful humorist Will Cuppy; it was titled *How to Attract the Wombat* and was something of a takeoff on the many books on how to attract birds. Now I have no objection to birds, or for that matter wombats or other forms of wild life: all are welcome on Wasp Farm. But we have been particularly anxious to attract wasps, and I would be remiss if I did not pass on a few pointers on a subject so vital to everyone. Or would you prefer a chapter on "How Not to Attract Wasps"?

I confess that now and then I would just as soon not attract certain wasps myself. A few yellow jackets add zest to a picnic, but too many make it a bit hazardous—and even I don't particularly like to eat wasps. But solitary wasps are another matter. The various digger wasps, mud daubers, and dwellers in twigs and rotten wood are a joy to have around.

Attracting wasps is not difficult; in fact, it is easier than not attracting them. One merely needs to be lazy. Let the weeds and brambles grow up, and don't prune the roses and fruit trees or cut out dead sumacs and elderberries: the more unkempt vegetation the more insects for wasps to prey upon, and the more hollow or pithy twigs the more cavities for them to nest in. Plow a garden and plant it to interesting things, but don't cultivate too conscientiously and by all means don't go overboard on insecticides: share the wealth with the insects, which after all are mostly attractive and rather amusing (even a worm in the salad provides interesting dinner conversation). Have a decrepit garage, woodshed, or out-house, and spare the paint and fancy new carpentry: many a wasp will use the eaves and various holes and crannies in the walls. And have a few barren places about, where the soil is loose, gravelly, and too poor to support anything but digger wasps.

Of course, if one's zeal is great enough, there are certain positive measures one can take to attract wasps, such as importing a sand dune. A much simpler project is to provide artificial nests for wasps that nest in hollow twigs. These can be crude or rather elaborate, depending upon one's inclination. The simplest type is easily made by taking stems of dead trees and shrubs (sumac is perhaps the best) and cutting them in lengths of six to ten inches. Some should have holes bored in one end, others left with the original pithy centers. They can then be tied singly or in bundles in trees or in the rafters of woodsheds or elsewhere. Certain wasps will use the bored out twigs, while other kinds will remove the pith and use those twigs. Some, if left undisturbed, will be used over and over again, sometimes by quite different species of wasps [or bees].

A somewhat neater type of "trap-nest" can be made by buying one-inch square strips of straight-grained, seasoned pine and cutting them in lengths of about six inches. Then, with a good assortment of long bits, drill a hole in one end of each for nearly the length of the stick. Differently sized bores between one-eighth and one-half inch in diameter attract wasps of different sizes. Trap-nests of this type can easily be mass-produced and scattered about single or in clusters in trees, sheds, or almost anywhere above ground, generally in a horizontal position. Filled nests can be spotted easily because the hole will have been closed off by the wasp with a plug of mud or vegetable matter. If one wishes to study the contents, the nest can be split open lengthwise with a jack-knife; the two sides can be put together again and held there by rubber bands. More elaborate types employ narrow sheets of glass beside the boring, the glass being covered by metal or wooden strips. Nests of this type can be examined without having to split the wood, but they are more expensive to make. ...

Artificial trap-nests have provided a wonderful boon to biologists interested in learning about the distribution of twig-nesting wasps and their behavior and that of their parasites. By saturating an area with trap-nests of varying bore diameter, one can obtain an idea of the species of twig-nesters present and the relative numbers of each, how they compete for nesting sites, how they differ with respect to nest structure and type of prey, what parasites are present and which wasps they attack, and so forth. Even a few trap-nests in a back yard provide an interesting spectacle for children and adults alike. ...

To a person attuned to them, like myself, the world seems full of wasps. I have never actually counted the species on Wasp Farm, but I would judge there are over one hundred that occur there fairly regularly. Karl Krombein, an entomologist at the Smithsonian Institution and one of the world's most noted authorities on wasps, has been making a census of the wasps found on Plummer's Island, a small, fourteen-acre island in the Potomac not far from Washington, D.C. So far he has recorded over 250 species, and the end is not yet in sight. And some species of wasps are incredibly abundant; I once estimated ten thousand individuals in a large nesting aggregation of sand wasps in southern Florida.

In spite of all this, it must be admitted that most wasps are relatively scarce, that nearly all of them nest rather obscurely, and that none of them make a very important impression upon man or upon the populations of the insects they prey upon. Most wasps seem simply to skim the cream off the abundance of nature, taking a small percentage of the most common of insects. Attempts to manipulate wasps in order to control pests have generally ended in failure; the only exception I know of is the case of the "Spanish Jack," a species of paper wasp that has been intentionally carried about in the West Indies and has been of some importance in reducing the populations of several species.

Perhaps, then, the story of wasp evolution is the story of a long road to failure. Perhaps the best that can be said for wasps is that at one point early in their history they gave rise to the ants, and at another point somewhat later on to the bees. Ants and bees are certainly not failures by any standards. Ants are probably the most abundant of all creatures on land, and they seem to carry on their manifold activities without being discouraged very much by man; in fact, some species thrive in his homes and gardens. As for the bees, without them we would be without most of the flowering plants, without many of our food crops. No matter what strange things man does to the face of the earth in the future, it is hard to imagine him getting along without bees to pollinate his crops.

We humans, of course, tend to define success in terms of dollars and cents, in terms of how big a "splash" is made in the world, in terms of how much the environment is molded to our ends. But other definitions are possible. If I were to define success as a harmonious living together with the environment, as a gradual unfolding into many small available places in nature, as a surviving for eons of time *without* making a great splash—then the wasps would qualify. But where would that leave man?

4

Ants, Elephants, and Men:
Strands from the Fabric
of Natural History

Mary Alice and I published this essay in American Scientist *in 1966. It was a spin-off from the preparation of our book* William Morton Wheeler, Biologist, *which the Harvard University Press published in 1970. Writing a biography was a new experience for us, but since we are "whodunit" addicts, we felt at home tracking down some of the intertwining threads of lives during a period of natural history that is too soon forgotten in our fast-moving times.*

WHEN P. T. BARNUM'S MUSEUM reopened on Broadway in New York in October 1860, its proprietor promised "a mysterious novelty never before seen in that establishment": no less than a cherry-colored cat. When his audience was primed, he pulled from the bag an ordinary black cat, explaining that it was, of course, "the color of black cherries." The audience roared, the newspaper reporters scuttled off with their stories, and Barnum had scored another triumph.

It was little wonder that when, a year later, Barnum ("There's a sucker born every minute") announced his newest exhibit, two rarely seen white whales, there were those who were skeptical. But as Barnum had launched a major expedition to the mouth of the St. Lawrence River to capture the whales, and had paid $4,000 to have a tank twenty-four feet square built to hold them, he was

21

determined that they should be certified as genuine white whales. No less a person than Professor Louis Agassiz of Harvard was induced to examine them. He announced that they were, indeed, white whales. Unfortunately the whales soon died, but even this was turned into a triumph for Barnum. Agassiz's endorsement was published far and wide and displayed for many years in the museum, and the tank was shortly thereafter used for "the first and only genuine hippopotamus that had ever been seen in America."

Barnum was to call on Professor Agassiz for help once again. This time the charge was cruelty to animals, leveled by Henry Bergh, one-time diplomat to Russia, founder of the American SPCA, a colorful crusader immortalized by Longfellow as "the friend of every friendless beast." Bergh himself had turned to Agassiz when seeking support for his campaign against cruelty to turtles. Agassiz, a turtle-lover, gladly complied with a testament on the suffering of turtles. But when Bergh stormed Barnum's Museum, loudly protesting the feeding of live rabbits to boa constrictors, it was Barnum who appealed to Agassiz. Agassiz was a snake-lover, too, and he pointed out that snakes will accept only living food. "I do not think the most active member of the Society," he wrote, "would object to eating lobster salad because the lobster was boiled alive ... or raw oysters because they must be swallowed alive." Barnum did oblige Bergh by feeding the snakes at night, thus sparing the public a scene the SPCA president regarded as "cruel and demoralizing."

While Barnum's showmanship was sometimes suspect, and perhaps with cause, that of Louis Agassiz was without taint. Trained under some of Europe's finest zoologists, he had come to Boston in 1846 as a visiting lecturer, and he had stayed to charm a nation and found a museum of rather different character from Barnum's. Like Barnum, Agassiz was sometimes embroiled in controversy. His theories of glaciation were not accepted by all, though history has shown him more right than wrong. Much of his later life was devoted to efforts to refute Darwinian evolution, and here history has not treated him kindly. Agassiz often chose the popular magazines, such as *The Atlantic Monthly*, for his essays on these and other subjects, for to him science was not something merely to be pursued in the dark corners of his museum. "The time has come," he said, "when scientific truth must cease to be the property of the few, when it must be woven into the common life of the world; for we have reached the point where the results of science touch the very problem of existence. ..." That was in 1862!

Agassiz was an imposing figure on the lecture platform. In the words of one contemporary: "He was strikingly handsome, with a dome-like head under flowing black locks, large, dark, mobile eyes set in features strong and comely. ..." Horace Greeley heralded his arrival in New York on a lecture tour by remarking in the *Tribune* that "never have our citizens enjoyed the opportunity of acquiring so large a measure of knowledge of the laws of nature ... as these lectures will afford them." Both scientist and layman were held spellbound as Agassiz discoursed on subjects as diverse as embryology, glaciation, and fossil fishes.

When Agassiz was scheduled to lecture in Rochester, New York, in January of 1854, a lad of twenty named Henry A. Ward hiked thirty miles from school through mud and snow to see and hear the famous naturalist. Ward, who had been interested in rocks and fossils for at least half of his life, was overjoyed the next morning when he was asked to show Agassiz the local geological points of interest. Agassiz was delighted with his day's excursion with Ward, and he promptly invited Ward to study with him at Harvard. During his apprenticeship with Agassiz, Ward first learned the value of museums in the advancement of scientific teaching and research. He went on to devote his life to providing specimens for museums, including Professor Agassiz's.

In the late eighteen hundreds, ordinary traveling was not easy, but Ward's desire to secure unusual specimens to supply the museums took him to many remote parts of the world. His reports home, when he found time to make them, must have made some of his friends wonder if his imagination was not rivaling Barnum's. One story told of a collecting trip in 1859, when Ward was barely twenty-five, on the Niger River in West Africa. He was taken ill with blackwater fever, then the scourge of the white man in the tropics, and the superstitious crew of the river boat put him ashore and left him to die. A native woman rescued him and nursed him back to health, with the clear intention of making him her husband. Somehow Ward managed to slip away and eventually to appear at his home in Rochester. Sometime later a large packing case of gifts was left by a passing ship on the bank by the hut of his dusky benefactress. Meanwhile, at a party in London, David Livingston was reported to have ignored many important guests so that he might converse with the young American who knew Africa so well.

Agassiz himself traveled widely, and his travels were closely followed by the press—usually with prose, but sometimes in rhyme. Oliver Wendell Holmes celebrated Agassiz's departure for Brazil with an ode beginning:

> May he find, with his apostles,
> That the land is full of fossils,
> That the waters swarm with fishes
> Shaped according to his wishes,
> That every pool is fertile
> In fancy kinds of turtle. ...

Agassiz's ability to raise money for his many scientific projects became legend even in his time. In early 1873, he conceived the idea of starting a summer school "somewhere on the coast of Massachusetts where teachers from our schools and colleges could make their vacations serviceable by the direct study of nature." John Anderson, a wealthy New Yorker, read the details of Agassiz's plan in the *Tribune*, and immediately presented him with the island of Penikese, in Buzzard's Bay, along with $50,000 for the founding of the school. As one contemporary put it, Agassiz had only to desire, and desire became reality.

Agassiz himself felt that he was primarily a teacher and that his greatest triumph was his summer school at Penikese. It was a pioneering effort both as a coeducational summer school and as a seaside laboratory. Although the physical plant was incomplete when the school opened in July, Agassiz declared that never had a laboratory been better equipped. The sea was abounding in life, the shore had in addition to its living inhabitants a great diversity of pebbles all with interesting stories to be revealed. Study nature, not books, was Agassiz's motto: I will only help you to discover what you want to know yourself. In retrospect, David Starr Jordan (later to become the first president of Stanford University) said: "The summer went on through a succession of joyous mornings, beautiful days, and calm nights, with the Master always present, always ready to help and encourage, the contagious enthusiasm which surrounded him like an atmosphere never lacking." The poet Whittier was moved to describe that remarkable summer in his poem beginning:

> On the isle of Penikese
> Ringed about by sapphire seas,
> Fanned by breezes salt and cool,
> Stood the Master with his school.

This was to be the last summer of Agassiz's life; when his group met again the next summer, but without their famed teacher, the magic was gone, and the Penikese school was never to be again. But many of the students at Penikese were to become leaders in biology, bringing fresh insight into the constant search for new truths. Perhaps James Russell Lowell sensed this, for he wrote after Agassiz's death: "He was a teacher; why be grieved for him whose living word still stimulates the air?"

One of the students at Penikese was Charles Otis Whitman, a high school teacher of quiet manners with, already at thirty, a shock of snow-white hair. Whitman was a Bowdoin College graduate, but it was not until his two summers at Penikese that he took up

biology in earnest. Like most biologists of his time, he went to
Europe to learn the latest theories and techniques, and like most
of his contemporaries he spent some time at the new biological
station at Naples, Italy. Built by a devoted German scientist on the
picturesque shore of the Bay of Naples, this gleaming white building, dedicated to science, has caused some to remark that not all
temples are built for the love of a beautiful woman.

In 1882, Whitman came back to the quiet, dusty alcoves of Mr.
Agassiz's museum at Harvard. This Mr. Agassiz was Alexander
Agassiz, son of Louis. For four years Whitman assisted Agassiz
with his studies of fish, but Whitman was destined to be much
more than an assistant. Then in his forties, he was ready for an opportunity to exercise his independence of spirit and to develop his
own ideals. That opportunity came when Whitman was asked to
direct a new research laboratory in the cultural center of the Mid-
west: Milwaukee, Wisconsin.

Milwaukee, a transported German city which had been built by
the intellectual refugees from an unsuccessful rebellion against
the German monarchies, had one of the best public schools in
the country, a public library, and a public natural history museum. The latter owed its existence to Henry A. Ward. At the Milwaukee Exposition of 1883, Professor Ward exhibited a portion
of his tremendous collection of stuffed animals in an effort to persuade the city fathers that a great and influential metropolis such
as theirs should have a public museum. It could be started easily,
he said, by purchasing his exhibit and combining it with the small
but good collections then at the local German-English Academy.
Ward was successful, not only in improving Milwaukee, but also
in saving his business, which needed this sale to keep from going
bankrupt. Someone else profited from the venture, too: a local
boy named William Morton Wheeler, a student at the German-
English school. Wheeler, classically trained but with an unusual
enthusiasm for things biological, had haunted the school museum
for years, and knew every specimen. When Ward arrived,

Wheeler was asked to help arrange the exhibits, and before long Ward had invited him to come and work for him in Rochester (New York) at his Establishment—for nine dollars a week minus six for room and board at Ward's own house.

Young Bill Wheeler's eagerness to work among the wonderful beasts in Rochester gave way to amazement when he saw Ward's Natural Science Establishment. Sixteen wooden buildings of various sizes, each with a gilded totem pole at its peak to show the nature of its contents, opened into a common court yard. As Wheeler entered the court, he passed beneath a Gothic arch formed by the jaws of a whale, and was confronted by a conspicuous placard:

> THIS IS NOT A MUSEUM
> But a Working Establishment
> Where All are Very Busy.

Slightly to the left was the main building, and on the door-step was a stuffed gorilla with an open, leering mouth, clinging to a naked tree trunk. A less determined young man might have fled. But in Ward's study, a room lined with books and littered with maps, sketches, and specimens, Wheeler was genuinely welcomed by his host.

Wheeler began his work with pleasure, identifying and listing birds and mammals, and later shells, but unfortunately Professor Ward, whom he so much admired, spent more time traveling than he did in Rochester. But there were a number of young men around, and in spite of the dictum outside they enjoyed many informal times together. Wheeler was especially attracted to a young taxidermist brought up on a farm not far from Rochester, Carl Akeley. The two spent many long evenings together, often with Wheeler reading aloud and Akeley working on his animals.

By the spring of 1885, both Wheeler and Akeley felt that there were better opportunities elsewhere. Wheeler wanted to go back to his cultural Milwaukee. He suggested to Akeley that if he would come, too, he would tutor him as preparation for entering a scientific school. Besides, there might be a job for him in the new municipal museum. Wheeler did return to Milwaukee, where he soon became involved in teaching and research and where he shortly came under the influence of C. O. Whitman at his laboratory. But an unexpected challenge kept Akeley at Rochester another year.

At about nine o'clock in the evening on September 15, 1885, at St. Thomas, Ontario, P. T. Barnum's seven-ton elephant, Jumbo, was being led along the railroad tracks to his car. Out of the night roared an unscheduled freight train. The locomotive struck Jumbo with terrific force, and within moments he was dead, the train derailed and badly damaged. The news was cabled all over the world, for Jumbo had been the greatest attraction Barnum had ever offered to the public. He had been bought at the astronomical price of $10,000 ($30,000 with carrying charges included!) from the Royal Zoological Gardens in London. Jumbo had been a favorite with the British, and there was great resentment at this transaction. It was rumored that even Queen Victoria tried to induce Barnum to take back his money and leave Jumbo in England. Jumbo was a sensation in America, and Barnum reputedly got back his money in ten days.

Not wanting to lose this asset, especially with the added publicity of the killing, Barnum decided to have Jumbo mounted. He wired Henry A. Ward, and Ward, Akeley, and a number of others rushed to the scene of the wreckage. With the aid of several local butchers, Jumbo's remains were removed as quickly as possible. It fell to Akeley mainly to oversee the feat of preserving Jumbo, so that the elephant could be put back on exhibition almost as though he could still breathe. This was done so well that Jumbo's massive skin still stands with all its life-like wrinkles, and his eyes still seem to stare out at those who come to see him in the foyer of the biology building at Tufts University. Jumbo's skeleton was mounted, too, and now is at the American Museum of Natural

History in New York. His heart, which weighed forty pounds, was advertised for sale by Ward for forty dollars. Who, if anyone, bought it no one seems to know.

When Jumbo was finished, Akeley followed Wheeler to Milwaukee, where he set up his taxidermy shop in Wheeler's barn. Shortly thereafter Wheeler was made director of the Milwaukee Public Museum, and Akeley joined the staff. There, under Wheeler's liberal and sympathetic leadership, Akeley created his first habitat group (which is still on exhibit)—a natural scene of muskrats in a pond. Wheeler helped Akeley start this project one cold October day in 1889, when the two walked shivering into a nearby swamp to gather the muskrat house and skins, and a few typical birds. To these, Akeley applied his new techniques of taxidermy, adding artifical reeds and water that he had devised, and created not only a remarkable illusion of muskrat activity, but a whole new concept in museum displays and public education.

Though Carl Akeley's skill was evident in Milwaukee, it was not until he began his studies of African animals that his great genius emerged. First, at the Field Museum in Chicago, and then at the American Museum of Natural History in New York, Akeley proved that he was much more than a mere taxidermist. To these museums he brought his knowledge of the out-of-doors and his ability to sculpture, creating for even the least informed audience a feeling for Africa and its unique wilderness. Akeley was especially fascinated by elephants, though once he was almost crushed by one. His dramatic group, "The Fighting Bulls," in Chicago was dwarfed only by his plans for his elephant group in New York. He wanted it to be part of a great African Hall, but unfortunately he did not live to complete his plans. He died on safari and was buried on the slopes of Mount Mikeno in the Congo—a spot he once called the most beautiful in the world. But his ideas were completed by workers whom he had trained, and the African exhibit today is dominated by the tremendous herd of elephants collected earlier by Akeley and his friend Theodore Roosevelt.

Thus, the Akeley Memorial African Hall stands as a tribute to a man of humble origins who cherished a dream to preserve for all to see an image of our dwindling wildlife in its natural setting.

The Milwaukee Public Museum and the nearby Allis Lake Laboratory were to provide the initial opportunity not only to Akeley and to Wheeler, but to several others who went on to distinguished careers. Although short-lived (seven years), the Lake Laboratory was a most unusual institution. It was founded by a businessman, Edward P. Allis, Jr. Pressured by his family to forsake his childhood interest in natural history, Allis was educated as an engineer so that he could enter the family business, the manufacture of farm machinery (later to become Allis-Chalmers). When he had proved himself as a businessman, he again took up the study of zoology in the few spare hours that he could get away from the factory. In a large billiard room on the third floor of his aunt's home near Lake Michigan, he set up a laboratory and then proceeded to seek a young and promising biologist as a director. He proposed to organize the laboratory like a business, wherein a group of specialists would work on a particular problem as a body and not as individuals. But Charles O. Whitman, the man he selected as director, had other ideas. Whitman believed that each worker should have absolute freedom of thought and action and should pursue his search for truth wherever it should lead. Whitman's ideas not only prevailed, but he soon persuaded Allis, who had no interest in publishing his research findings, to help organize and finance the *Journal of Morphology*, which was to be a model of excellence for all scientific periodicals.

Whitman was a soft-spoken man of simple tastes, throughout his life completely absorbed by his teaching and research. Nevertheless, beneath his quiet and kindly exterior was a brilliant and original mind and a fiercely independent spirit. In 1888, he was appointed the first director of the Marine Biological Laboratory at Woods Hole, Massachusetts—in many ways a lineal descendant of Penikese and of the Lake Laboratory. There for almost every summer for twenty years, Whitman directed the laboratory according to his ideals of cooperation of individuals and institutions, but with independence in government so that investigators could follow their own research with complete freedom. The stature of the laboratory today may be attributed largely to Whitman's genius.

The challenge of founding a biological station might have been all an ordinary man could handle, but Dr. Whitman had another equally exciting offer at about the same time. The new Clark University in Worcester, Massachusetts, was to be solely a graduate and research institution, and in 1889 Whitman was asked to come and direct the department of zoology. There was little formal instruction, and each student was expected to work independently on his own particular problem. Yet no one was permitted to become a specialist completely. Whitman, as had Professor Agassiz, encouraged his students not to allow anything their animals did to escape attention. Thus Whitman's students were reported to greet each other not with "What is your special field?" but rather "What is your beast?"

One of Whitman's most enthusiastic students was William Morton Wheeler. Wheeler had come under Whitman's influence first at the Lake Laboratory, and he had followed him to Clark, where he completed his graduate studies in 1892. He then left Clark, along with Whitman and others. Once more Whitman had been asked to organize a new biology department. This time it was at the new University of Chicago, and there Whitman remained, except for summers at Woods Hole, becoming one of the country's foremost students of animal behavior. His classic monograph on the behavior of pigeons was published posthumously in 1919.

If Charles Otis Whitman was a credit to the ability of his teacher, Louis Agassiz, then William Morton Wheeler was no less so for Whitman. In 1899, Wheeler left Chicago, after several years of teaching there, to direct the department of zoology at the University of Texas at Austin. After the many years of rich academic associations and atmospheres, Texas seemed virtually a wilderness frontier. There were few books and little laboratory equipment available in the university, and Wheeler was faced with the formidable task of not only teaching the beginning course in zoology, but also most of the advanced ones. Discouraged at the prospect of so much to do and so little with which to do it, Wheeler took his lunch one day and went out to eat it in a dry stream bed near the campus. Passing near him in steady procession were long lines of ants carrying leaves. He watched them with puzzled fascination for a while, and then said to himself: these are worth a lifetime of study! Wheeler went on to become a world authority on ants—the most abundant of all animals on earth, as Wheeler himself often pointed out.

For four years Wheeler directed the zoological studies at the University of Texas, even organizing a short-lived marine laboratory on the Gulf coast. Then he was challenged anew at the prospect of reorganizing the invertebrate animal collections at the American Museum of Natural History. After five productive years in New York, he was appointed to a professorship at Harvard, where he spent the remainder of his life.

Wheeler was a brilliant writer and lecturer, a man of encyclopedic learning. He could and did discourse on the most abstruse philosophical matters, yet some of his essays find their way regularly into the anthologies of popular natural history. In one of these papers he wrote: "Natural history constitutes the perennial rootstock or stolon of biological science ... because it satisfies some of our most fundamental and vital interests in organisms as living individuals more or less like ourselves." In the same essay he staunchly supported the amateur in a characteristic Wheelerism: "The truth is that the amateur naturalist radiates interest and enthusiasm as easily and copiously as the professor radiates dry-rot." A few lines later he excluded "dear old, mellow, disinfected professors of the type of Louis Agassiz ... [who could] enter at once into sympathetic rapport with the humblest amateur. ..." Wheeler had made his point—one worth reiterating in these times, when the amateur is so frequently barred from the halls of science.

Like Agassiz, Wheeler was many things to many people. To Alfred North Whitehead, the Harvard philosopher, he was the only man he had ever known "who would have been both worthy and able to sustain a conversation with Aristotle." William Beebe characterized him as "an outstanding example of one who fulfilled every requirement of scientist, investigator, naturalist and literary master." To one of Wheeler's neighbors at his summer home in Colebrook, Connecticut: "Oh yes, there's Professor Wheeler. He comes up here every summer and turns over all the stones in the pasture and then he goes back to Boston."

In his later years, Wheeler became a regular inhabitant of the Agassiz Museum, and his ant collection, comprising more than a million specimens from all parts of the world, is one of the most valued treasures of that institution.

Thus the wheel has come full circle—or rather several circles. And who can trace fully the many strands of thought which connected these men and their students? All were individualists, often of very different temperament; yet through them all runs a common strand, a fascination with animals as living beings. In these days of specialization and depersonalization, in these times of the two cultures and the scientific elite, we look back upon these expansive and independent spirits with incredulity, sometimes with amusement. Animals were to each of them the touchstone, and their lives were intertwined with those of ants and elephants and other living things. Today biology, like every other human activity, is caught up in a whirlwind. Personally, we would hope never quite to lose sight of men such as Agassiz discoursing on fossil fishes to an audience of spellbound laymen, of Whitman surrounded by his pigeons, of Wheeler watching a column of ants—yes, even of Barnum perpetrating some new extravaganza, of Henry A. Ward offering Jumbo's heart for forty dollars. By the way, what *did* become of Jumbo's heart?

5

First on the Wind

*In 1975, Stephen Dalton brought together his remarkable photographs of insects
in flight in a volume published by the Reader's Digest Press, titled* Borne on the
Wind. *I was asked to write a Foreword, published later that year in* Audubon
*under the title "First on the Wind." For indeed insects were on the wing long be-
fore birds and bats appeared. They are still on the wing, as recalled by the Spanish proverb "En una boca cerrada, no entran moscas."*

THE FLIGHT OF INSECTS has intrigued curious persons since
the time of Leonardo da Vinci, and doubtless before. Leonardo
and, almost two centuries later, Giovanni Borelli propounded a
number of aerodynamic principles, though they based most of
their conclusions on the study of birds. Even Louis Agassiz, after
the passage of another two centuries, incorrectly supposed that
the wings of butterflies and moths became separated during the
upstroke, allowing air to pass between them as it does between
the primaries of birds.

With increasing knowledge of insect anatomy, and particularly
with the invention of high-speed motion picture photography,
the unique properties of insect flight gradually became more apparent, for insects are too small and their wingbeat too fast to permit many conclusions from direct observations. Still there remained many controversies. Puzzlement over the mechanics of
insect flight led certain researchers to conclude that some new
principles must be involved, and this led to the often repeated

35

(but not quite correct) statement that biologists have proved that insects really can't fly!

Then there was the episode concerning an American entomologist who, as recently as 1926, watched deer botflies flying past him with such speed that they were, in his words, "only a blur or streak of color." He also estimated their speed at 820 miles an hour (more than the speed of sound), a report so remarkable that it reached the pages of *The New York Times* and the *Illustrated London News*. Twelve years later the chemist Irving Langmuir calculated that propelling a fly at this speed would consume fuel so rapidly that the whole insect would burn up in half a second. And if a botfly hit a person at that speed it would penetrate with the force of a bullet! In fact, we now know that botflies, although among the fastest of insects, achieve a speed of no more than about 25 miles per hour.

Fortunately we are now well past the stage when anyone is likely to make so gross a miscalculation, but insect flight is still a very active field of research. We know, for example, that the exceedingly rapid contractions of the flight muscles generate considerable heat, so that the temperature inside the thorax— the middle section of the body which bears the wings and legs— is sometimes more than 30 degrees Celsius above the outside temperature. In fact, such heavy-bodied insects as bumblebees and hawk moths require flight muscle temperatures of 30 to 40 degrees C before sufficient lift can be produced to support them in flight. This raises some serious questions: How do they prevent overheating? And how do they manage to take off when the air temperature is below 30 to 40 degrees C (86 to 104 degrees Fahrenheit)?

Bernd Heinrich of the University of California at Berkeley [now at the University of Vermont] recently showed that when the dorsal blood vessel of a hawk moth is tied off just behind the thorax, the thorax does, in fact, overheat, so that the moth cannot be induced to continue flying. Evidently the blood passing

back from the thorax is cooled in the abdomen before being returned to the flight muscles. And it has been known for some
time that heavy-bodied insects such as hawk moths and giant
silkworm moths must warm up their flight muscles by "shivering" before they are able to take flight. It is noteworthy that those
insects in which temperature regulation is critically important
have bodies densely clothed with scales and hairs, providing a
measure of insulation.

The flight of the bumblebee is a particularly remarkable per-
formance. It is no coincidence that the person who set it to music,
Nikolai Rimski-Korsakov, was a Russian, for bumblebees are
especially characteristic of northern climes and in fact nest successfully north of the Arctic Circle. Even when temperatures are
barely above freezing, they are able to achieve and maintain an
internal temperature of more than 30 degrees C. Bumblebees
weigh only one to six-tenths of a gram, and for an organism so
small to produce so much heat requires a prodigious expenditure
of energy, which is fueled by nectar from flowers or honey from
the pots in their nests. Bernd Heinrich and his coworkers have
shown that the bumblebee is somehow able to uncouple its wings
from its flight muscles when it is stationary, so that it can vibrate
the muscles and thus warm up without actually moving the wings.
Bumblebees, like some other bees and wasps, also use body heat
so generated to raise the temperature of the larvae and pupae in
their nests.

Although bumblebees do not have a great many predators,
there is no doubt that many moths that require a prolonged warm-
up before flight are especially vulnerable to attacks by birds. It is
noteworthy that many of these moths, such as hawk moths and
giant silkworm moths, have large eyespots on their wings. It has
been shown experimentally that these eyespots do, in fact, have
survival value in frightening off birds, especially when combined
with the shivering movements that are prerequisite to flight. The
British behaviorist A. D. Blest showed that artificial eyespots, when

painted on quite abnormal subjects, such as mealworms, greatly reduced the rate of predation by several kinds of birds.

All of this serves to remind us that insects use their wings for many purposes other than flight. Some moths frighten predators with eyespots; other moths and many other insects have wing shapes and colors that blend with the background, rendering them virtually invisible. Many butterflies have spots along the edge of the wing which serve as deflection marks, inducing birds to nip them there rather than in more vulnerable parts of the body. Some of the hairstreak butterflies even have a "false head" formed from the back part of the hindwing, presumably causing birds no end of confusion.

We tend to think of the scales of a moth's wing as serving primarily to produce the color pattern. But Thomas Eisner of Cornell University has shown that the relatively loose scales of the wings of small moths enable them to escape from spiders' webs and from insectivorous plants such as sundews. When captured, they merely struggle a bit and work their way out, leaving a few scales behind.

Above all, one thinks of the many ways that wings are used to provide signals that assist in bringing the sexes together—and reproduction is, after all, what insects are best at. Even as I write this, in November, short-horned grasshoppers are clattering in my back yard, the wing sounds of the males still hopeful despite the imminence of snow. In male crickets and katydids the front wings are greatly modified for producing some of the most remarkable sounds in the animal kingdom.

Even the simple wing sounds of midges and mosquitoes play a role in bringing the sexes together. In this case it is the female that attracts the male by the hum of her wings, a fact quickly apparent to singers who hit a G in the vicinity of a swarm and end up with a mouthful of male mosquitoes. Certain male fruit flies use their wings to fan toward the female a chemical sex attractant produced by their glands. Many male butterflies have parts of their wings covered with specialized scales that produce substances attractive to the females. When these are removed, the males court even more vigorously, but with frustrating results.

Wing colors may also play a role in courtship, but less often than one might think, for most insects are better smellers than they are seers. One exception is provided by the dragonflies and damselflies, which have huge eyes and very small antennae. Here we know that colors and the translucence of flickering wings do play a role in courtship. In butterflies there are subtleties we have only just begun to appreciate. Robert Silberglied of Harvard University, along with several coworkers, found that the males of certain yellow "sulfur" butterflies have patches of scales that reflect ultraviolet light. These patterns are invisible to us under normal conditions, but insects perceive ultraviolet, and it is clear that these patterns play a role in bringing together the two sexes of one species.

The wings of certain insects even play a role in the mating act itself. In at least one species of cricket, the female consumes the wings of the male during copulation. Perhaps the most remarkable instance of the use of the wings during mating involves a curious species of scorpionfly that occurs on patches of moss during the colder times of the year. These insects are flightless, the females having no wings at all and the male having wings that are somewhat rodlike, with a hook at the end. The male uses these hooks to seize the female and later to hold her in the proper position for copulation. But by far the most important function of wings is to fly, and in this respect insect wings are unique in at least two major ways. For one, there are no muscles in the wings as such, and all the power and control emanate from the body. For another, insect wings are not modified limbs as they are in birds and bats, and as they were in pterodactyls, but entirely new structures arising from the back—a feature, as some wag has pointed out, that insects share only with angels.

Insects had been airborne for many millions of years before birds and bats appeared and began to exploit them. These aerial predators presented not so much a threat as a challenge to insects, resulting in the evolution of swifter and more efficient flight patterns, as well as special mechanisms for avoiding capture. Bats, it is well known, emit ultrasonic chirps which bounce off objects in their path and inform them of the presence of obstacles as well as potential prey. Several groups of moths have responded by developing receptors for ultrasound. Kenneth Roeder and his associates at Tufts University have shown that these moths not only detect the bats' sonar but respond by abruptly changing their course of flight, thus frequently avoiding capture. Tiger moths have carried this one step further, having themselves developed the ability to produce ultrasonic clicks. These are produced in response to those of the bat, and evidently tell the bat "I am not good to eat," for in fact these moths have also developed nauseous fluids that render them distasteful.

Of course, all of the many repellent secretions, warning colors, mimicry, and protective resemblances of insects have evolved in response to predation by various of those johnny-come-latelies—birds, bats, lizards, shrews, and the like. Certain species of flies not only resemble yellowjackets closely in shape and color but even exhibit audio mimicry, producing an identical hum when they fly because the rate of wingbeat is identical. It has been shown experimentally that birds avoid yellowjackets because of their sting and thereafter avoid other insects resembling them.

How did insects first evolve those unique structures, the wings, and evolve them so early in geologic time? Here we enter another area of controversy, and one that is not likely to be resolved right away. When I was a student I learned that there were two theories: the flying-squirrel theory, that wings arose as flat outgrowths first used for gliding; and the flying-fish theory, that wings were originally platelike gills that were used for flopping about on land when the primeval freshwater pools dried up. The latter view is suggested by a look at the immature stages of mayflies, which today have platelike gills on the abdomen that are moved by muscles. But the flying-squirrel theory has been much more popular down through the years and is supported by the fact that some of the ancient fossil insects have broad flaps on the back of the thorax that look like gliding surfaces and incipient wings. Still another theory has been proposed by Richard Alexander, of the University of Michigan, and William Brown, of Cornell. They believe that wings may have arisen in a terrestrial environment and as accessories to mating. Perhaps they were originally flaps to cover certain glands on the back that produced a sex attractant (as in tree crickets today); they may then have become enlarged and brilliantly colored, providing an advertisement in courtship and territorial defense analogous to the dewlap of many lizards. Since this theory was proposed, it has been learned that some of the very earliest insects preserved as fossils did, indeed, have vivid color patterns on their wings. Wherever the truth may lie, it is obvious that the acquisition of wings unlocked a whole new world for insects, which might otherwise have remained as insignificant a part of the environment as, for example, their relatives the centipedes. We believe there may be a million species or more, and, according to one estimate, the total insect population of the Earth at any one time is a billion billion. Insects occur from Antarctica to well north of the Arctic Circle; from deep in the soil and the bottoms of deep lakes to the tops of high mountains and more than two miles high in the air. Even the most remote oceanic islands have a rich insect fauna.

It was once believed that much of the dispersal of insects was the result of accidental drifting about in air currents. We now know that there are episodes in the life cycle of many insects, often soon after they acquire their wings and adult reproductive organs, when they deliberately launch themselves into the air and undertake flight patterns likely to take them to appropriate places to feed and reproduce. When there are mass flights of large insects, such as locusts, we can well appreciate them; but the migrations of plant lice, thrips, and myriad other small insects go largely unnoticed except by the specialist. The migration and dispersal of insects by flight is such a large and developing field of research that it took C. G. Johnson of the Rothamsted Experimental Station in England a book of 763 pages to survey the field, and doubtless he would be the first to admit that much more could be said on the subject.

The distances that insects are able to fly border on the incredible. Mosquitoes and blackflies may occasionally range as much as 50 to 100 miles from their breeding places, when aided by the wind and when they are able to refuel by feeding on nectar along the way. Some insects are capable of long, sustained flights without refueling; flights of dragonflies have, for example, been sighted many hundreds of miles at sea. The most remarkable, well-documented long-distance flight of an insect concerns the small mottled willow moth, which invaded England in great numbers in May 1962. Using data gathered by his staff and by amateur entomologists, combined with a study of weather maps for the period just preceding the invasion, C. B. Williams determined that the moths had traveled nonstop over the sea from Morocco, a distance of about 2,000 miles, in four days.

Despite all this, the average person is barely aware that insects exist at all, except perhaps for the fly that trespasses on his patio or the aphids that speckle his house plants. Stephen Dalton has developed a method of taking color photographs of insects in free flight, untethered and without artificial stimulation—the first successful undertaking of its kind. He would like to convince you that insects do indeed exist, that as flying machines they are unique as a group, yet diverse almost beyond belief, and above all, that they are things of unsurpassed beauty. I, for one, have always been willing to put up with occasional mosquito bites and wormy apples, such is my respect for the creatures that cause them, and such is my hope for a world of coexistence not only among men but among all living things.

6

The Intellectual and Emotional World of the Cockroach

Harper's ran this tribute to the cockroach in December 1966. Friends suggested that I add a few more favorite insects and put them in book form. The result was Life on a Little-known Planet, *which appeared in 1968 and led to my one appearance on television (the* Today *show). It has been reprinted four times in paperback, and as of this writing is still in print (The Lyons Press, New York). There were also two Japanese printings and one each in England, France, and Germany. All the world loves a cockroach.*

EVER SINCE ARCHY STOPPED jumping on the keys of Don Marquis' typewriter in the offices of the *New York Sun*, cockroaches have passed from the ken of most of us. It is a pity. Ours is a world of insecticides, rodenticides, herbicides, and etceticides. As archy complained, on reading an advertisement for a roach exterminator:

> the human race little knows
> all the sadness it
> causes in the insect world. ...

Of course, a biologist will tell you that insects are unlikely to experience sadness. But the human species is bereaved when it is unable to appreciate the world of small and creeping things. I heartily recommend cockroaches. Unlike archy, the average roach has little or no poetry in his soul. But he is a marvelous beast nonetheless. He must, of course, be met on his own terms, in his own world. He has been inhabiting that world successfully for somewhat more than 250 million years. The earliest fossil cockroaches look so much like contemporary species that one can almost imagine them freshly crushed by some irate housewife. But the first housewife was still more than 249 million years in the future. Any creature so adept at survival would seem to be worth our attention; survival is a subject we can stand to learn a lot more about.

Cockroaches are primarily creatures of the tropics and subtropics; in temperate regions we know them mainly from a few species that have found an easy living in our homes, stores, and restaurants. These domestic species include among others the American, German, Oriental, Surinam, and Cuban cockroach (a house my family once rented in Florida was a veritable United Nations of roachdom). A few years ago a cockroach was served to me in an order of beefsteak and onions in Texas (I believe it was American, but accurate identification of fried specimens is difficult). I was ravenously hungry after a day in the desert, so I ate everything except the cockroach, which I spread out neatly in the center of the empty plate, arranging his antennae and legs as best I could. The expression on the waiter's face when he cleared the table was ample compensation for the health risk I took. Although cockroaches are basically clean animals, they do track about a good deal of human filth; some carry bacteria responsible for various intestinal disorders, as well as polio virus and hookworm.

The names of our domestic roaches are largely the result of chance. When the Swedish naturalist Linnaeus received a roach from America he called it *americana*, while a roach from Asia he called *orientalis*. Even by that time (1758) most domestic cockroaches had spread over much of the globe, and modern transportation has finished the job. The late James A. G. Rehn, of the Academy of Natural Sciences of Philadelphia, revealed that the

American roach and its close relative the Australian roach belong to a group which occurs in the wild primarily in tropical Africa. He felt that these species, along with the Madeira roach and several others, came to America at an early date on slave ships. The Oriental roach also has wild relatives in Africa, but it arrived in Europe very long ago, perhaps on Phoenician vessels. Later it apparently traveled to South America on Spanish galleons and to North America on English ships.

The German roach, according to Rehn, came from North Africa. As it spread across Europe it was called the "Prussian roach" by the Russians, the "Russian roach" by the Prussians, thus paralleling the history of syphilis, which was known as the "French disease" throughout much of Europe, but as the "Italian disease" in France. The first outbreak of syphilis in the British colonies, by the way, occurred in Boston twenty-six years after the landing of the *Mayflower*. Evidently that noble ship and its immediate followers carried a good many things besides bluebloods, including, no doubt, the German roach, long an inhabitant of Boston slums but now fighting a rearguard action against urban renewal and the more recently arrived brown-banded cockroach.

America does, of course, have native roaches, but few of them have become domesticated, perhaps a reflection of the fact that man himself had his origins in Africa, thus giving the African roaches a big head start. The so-called Surinam roach apparently did not come originally from that Dutch colony in South America; Rehn found its closest relatives in the Orient, whence the species apparently spread to Africa and then joined several other species in slave ships traveling to that brave new world, America. Only one species, the so-called pale-bordered cockroach, has reversed the usual direction of immigration (may I say encroachment?) and reached the Canary Islands from its home in the West Indies.

Biologists are always on the lookout for animals easy to rear in the laboratory, and what could be easier than cockroaches, which are usually there to start with anyway. Most species require no more than a warm and cozy cage, a little water, and an occasional dog biscuit. Best of all, cockroaches—whom no one seems to love greatly—are exempt from most if not all of the bills pending in Congress which attempt to regulate and restrict the use of laboratory animals.

Scientists have used cockroaches in basic studies of animal behavior, nutrition, and metabolism, and even in cancer research. Dr. Berta Scharrer of the Albert Einstein College of Medicine found that when she cut certain nerves in the Madeira roach they developed tumors in some of the organs supplied by those nerves. Other workers have found tumors resulting from hormonal imbalance after transplanting endocrine glands in roaches. The application of these findings to the understanding of cancer in humans remains to be seen.

Behavior studies suggest that roaches are among the "brighter" insects. This was demonstrated in 1912 by C. H. Turner of Sumner Teachers College in Saint Louis, whose ingenious studies of animal behavior, often with homemade equipment, earned him a reputation as one of the leading negro biologists of his time. Turner, for example, tried "teaching machines" on cockroaches long before they came to be used for humans. He put roaches in cages containing two compartments, one lighted and one dark. True to their well-known preferences, Turner's roaches regularly headed for the dark compartment. However, when he wired it in such a way that they received an electric shock upon entering, they soon learned to go straight into the lighted compartment. (The males, he found, learned somewhat more quickly than the females.)

Turner also taught his cockroaches to run mazes successfully, a trick few insects can master. He rigged up a complex pattern of pathways made of copper strips supported over a pan of water. At the end of one runway was an inclined plane leading to the jelly glass that was "home" to that particular roach. After only five or six trials at half-hour intervals, most roaches reached their jars faster and faster and made fewer errors en route. In the course of a day the number of errors declined to almost zero. Turner's Oriental roaches had short memories and had to be retrained every day, but another worker found that American roaches remembered and even improved from day to day. Another researcher tried running two or three roaches together to see if they could solve a maze more rapidly in company—as certain fishes can. Exactly the opposite occurred. Apparently extracurricular distractions conflict with serious training even among roaches.

Lest anyone be inclined to dub the roaches "eggheads," I hasten to add that roaches *without* their heads are able to learn some things well. Recently Professor G. A. Horridge, of St. Andrews University in Scotland, arranged a decapitated roach in such a way that the legs received electric shocks every time they fell below a certain level. After about thirty minutes the roach changed its behavior in such a way that the legs were raised and few shocks were received. A decapitated roach, by the way, often lives for several days, although it eventually starves to death.

Doubtless the learning abilities of roaches have something to do with their success in putting up with the shenanigans of mankind. Other reasons for their success are to be found in their ability to scuttle off rapidly into crevices where they remain remarkably alert to peril. The roach's alarm system consists of long and active antennae on his head, and a pair of similar but shorter structures at the other end of the body, called *cerci* (from the Greek word for tails). These cerci are highly sensitive structures, and a light puff of air directed at one will send the roach scurrying. The cerci are covered with tiny hairs that bend when a current of air strikes them. Deflection of the hairs stimulates some of the many nerves in the cerci, which send a message to two clusters of nerve cells at their base. Here the message is transferred to giant fibers many times larger than ordinary nerve fibers. Giant fibers carry nerve impulses more than ten times as fast as ordinary nerves (the rate is more than 15 feet per second, which means that an impulse can traverse a giant fiber of the American roach in less than .003 seconds). These fibers carry the impulse directly to the nerves and muscles of the legs and produce the immediate escape response so characteristic of roaches.

To study the evasive behavior of the cockroach, Professor Kenneth Roeder of Tufts University rigged up a treadmill attached to a very sensitive recording device. Behind the roach on the treadmill, he placed a small tube through which a jet of air could be blown at the cerci. At the same time the air jet would strike a small paper flag, also connected to the recording device, such that the interval between the air jet and leg movements was registered. The cockroaches were fairly uncooperative, as experimental animals often are, and frequently cleaned themselves or made other unscheduled movements. But eventually Roeder obtained twenty-three good measurements which averaged about .05 seconds from air puff to leg movements. In subsequent experiments he found out why, although transmission over the giant fibers requires only about .003 seconds, another .047 seconds, more or less, are required for the final response. Some of the difference was caused by "synaptic delays," that is, the time taken for the impulse to cross from one nerve to another.

Synapses are the switchboards of the nervous system and provide the major means of sorting and directing messages. They do slow things down. Because giant fibers bypass many synapses, they speed up the response. A number of ordinary nerve fibers might handle more information than one giant fiber but at the cost of several thousandths of a second. In the course of evolution, this small gain in speed of escape from enemies outweighed the importance of carrying more detailed messages.

Our own human warning systems operate on much the same principle: emphasis is on rapid transmission of simple messages ("missile approaching") rather than much slower transmission of analytical reports. Such a system may have enhanced the survival of roaches as a group by millions of years, for their response is quick escape, and if the source of stimulation is in fact harmless, nothing is lost. *Our* problem, since we have no place to escape to, is to avoid an inappropriate response to meaningless information.

In addition to their gift for speedy retreat, some roaches have developed effective defense mechanisms. They can spray would-be predators with repellent chemicals. Dr. Thomas Eisner of Cornell University has found that one spray—known as a quinone—caused attacking ants and beetles to retreat and to undergo "a series of abnormal seizures, during which the leg movements became discoordinated and ineffectual." (Quinones similar to those produced by certain cockroaches have bactericidal properties, and may some day conceivably find a role as medical antibiotics.)

At least one roach has wholly abandoned cowardice in favor of aggression. This roach, with the suitably frightening name *Gromphadorhina portentosa*, not only produces an odor but makes a loud, hissing sound when disturbed. The males are sometimes as much as four inches long and have a pair of thick horns just behind their heads. When males chance upon one another they charge and push each other back and forth with their horns, all the while hissing loudly. This roach is a native of Madagascar and has not become domesticated, thank God; it is not the sort of thing one would want to encounter on the kitchen shelf.

The lives of cockroaches are remarkably automated. Apparently they don't even have to rely on their senses to decide when to go out on their nightly prowls. This was demonstrated by Dr. Janet Harker of Cambridge University, England, who found that American roaches kept in constant darkness nevertheless became more active when it was night outside, at least for a period of several days. Apparently a hormone is released from a group of cells in the head every twenty-four hours and "tells" the roach to bestir itself. A beheaded cockroach can't tell the time of day— not because he has no eyes but because he has lost the glands which produce this hormone. When Dr. Harker implanted a gland that was producing the hormone rhythmically, she could restore the rhythm of activity in the headless roach. By subjecting the gland to temperatures close to freezing, she was able to "reset the clock." However, this could be done only with a transplanted gland; when left in the original roach, the gland resets itself. It isn't quite clear why cockroaches need a system for "instrument takeoffs" when they can tell when it is dark by simply looking out of their crevices.

Like other insects, roaches have no hormones produced by their sex organs. They hardly need them, adult insects being designed for reproduction and not much else. They do have certain built-in inhibiting devices, however; insects cannot afford to spend *all* their waking hours in sex, phonetics notwithstanding. We know that certain endocrine glands in the head of a female roach have much influence on the formation of her eggs. In some species, if these glands are removed soon after the female becomes sexually mature, she fails to produce a chemical—known as a pheromone—which attracts males, and is therefore very likely doomed to spinsterhood. But if she is doused with sex attractant taken from normal females, she can attract males and mates in the usual manner. When a female Surinam roach is pregnant, pressure of the developing eggs sends a nervous impulse to the head which suppresses these same glands and thus stops production of the sex attractant until the eggs are laid.

Many other insects produce pheromones, and the study of their chemistry and effects is currently a very active field of biology. In some cockroaches, the male must actually contact the female before being stimulated, while in other cases the pheromone attracts males from a distance.

The German roach has paid for its intimacy with man by having its sex life analyzed in great detail. When a male detects the pheromone of a female, he faces the intended spouse and the pair begin to "fence" with their antennae. Shortly thereafter he turns completely around and faces away from her, at the same time raising his wings at about a 90-degree angle. Through this gesture he is offering her his own chemical attractants, which exude from glands on his back. If courtship is proceeding well, the female climbs upon his back and begins to feed on these exudates, which lure her into copulating position. After a few seconds the male begins to push himself farther back beneath the female, at the same time extruding his genital organs. These are extraordinary structures, resembling nothing so much as a Boy Scout jackknife, with its various blades and bottle and can openers. With the longest of these hooks the male clamps onto a small crescent-shaped plate at the tail end of the female. Then he moves out from under her and turns about facing away from her. Other, smaller hooks are then attached to other structures on the female, who is literally "hooked" for the hour or two required for copulation.

Dr. Louis Roth, [formerly] of the U.S. Army Laboratories in Natick, Massachusetts, has found important differences in the reproductive behavior of various species. The American roach is more direct than the German, pushing himself beneath the female with hardly any preliminaries. In this species and many others, males are greatly stimulated by female sex pheromones even in the absence of females. If filter paper is taken from the bottom of a cage of females and placed in a cage of males, the latter become greatly excited, flutter their wings, and attempt to mate with the paper. Workers at the United States Department of Agriculture have succeeded in isolating the sex attractant of the American roach by passing a stream of air through jars containing thousands of females, collecting the vapor by freezing it with dry ice. In nine months, they obtained 12.2 milligrams (about .0004 ounces) of this substance, which proved to be intensely exciting to males.

Dr. Robert Barth of the University of Texas, who has become something of a Sigmund Freud to the roach world, finds that homosexuality is rare among roaches. However, he reports that when female pheromone is introduced into a cage of male Cuban roaches, they tear about their cage and proceed to court one another furiously. All steps in heterosexual courtship can be seen, except of course the final hooking together of the genitalia. We still know very little about the actual nature of these potent sex attractants. Perhaps it is just as well.

The eggs of roaches are produced in neat little packets which, in our homes and laboratory cages, are simply dropped on the floor, to hatch some time later if they do not dry up or become food for another roach. But we now know that this behavior is the result of an abnormal environment. In their natural habitats most roaches safeguard the next generation by concealing their eggs.

I watched one method in a Florida state park on a warm spring evening several years ago. Around me were several female giant Florida roaches—a brown, wingless, and rather odorous species that has not become domesticated to any extent. Each had an egg case protruding from the end of her body, and each was digging a hole in the sand or at least looking for a place to dig. When she had selected a suitable spot she made a series of backward strokes with her head, piling the sand beneath and behind her. After the hole was about a third of an inch deep, she dribbled saliva into it, picked up the moistened sand grains with her mouth and eventually molded a trough-shaped cavity of proper size and shape to fit the egg capsule. Next she straddled the pit, released the egg case, and slid it into the hole with movements of her abdomen, turning around and making final adjustments with her mandibles. Then she plastered moistened sand over the top of the egg case and smoothed it over. Finally, after more than an hour of hard work, she wandered off into the darkness, having effectively protected against predators, parasites, and desiccation of offspring she would never see herself.

In laboratory cages, this same roach, like other species, merely drops her egg cases on the floor. But if she is provided with sand, she will act out her normal egg-burying behavior (to a bleary-eyed audience, sometime in the middle of the night).

Other roaches have quite different methods of protecting their eggs. The German roach, for example, carries her egg case around, projecting from the end of her body, and even transfers water to it. She drops it when the eggs are ready to hatch. The female Madeira and Surinam roaches, after extruding the egg case, draw it back into the body, where it occupies a special brood sac until hatching occurs. These roaches are unique in being "born twice," since the eggs first leave the body of the female and are then drawn back in, to emerge the second time as young roaches. In the brood sac, the eggs are thoroughly protected and are supplied with water and, in at least one case, with nutriment. The Surinam roach has even dispensed with the nuisance of having a male sex; one strain of this species consists entirely of females which produce live female young, which grow up to produce live female young, and so on *ad infinitum.* If there is a more efficient reproductive mechanism, the roaches will undoubtedly find it.

When a scientist is asked what good his research is, the classic answer (and a good one) is a shrug of the shoulders. To a student of roaches, it is self-evident that any creature so beautifully adapted and adaptable is worth lifetimes of study. If there are any underlying principles of long-term survival, surely they are evidenced by the roaches. Of the 3,500 species now living, fewer than 5 per cent have been studied in any detail. What we do know suggests that every species is a story in itself, and that even our best-known species have still to yield final answers to many details of body function. The study of roaches may lack the aesthetic values of bird-watching and the glamour of space flight, but nonetheless it would seem to be one of the more worthwhile human activities. In fact, as I scan the evening paper, I wonder if it may not be more worthwhile than most of them.

7

In Defense of Magic:
The Story of Fireflies

This essay has been lifted twice from its place as a chapter in Life on a Little-known Planet, *once in* Natural History, *November 1968, and once in* Bowen and Mazzeo's *book* Writing About Science *(1979). Alas, fireflies do not occur near our present home, but last summer we camped in a remote canyon in southeastern Colorado and at dusk we found the valley filled with dancing lights. Had we found gold in the canyon, it would have been dross by comparison.*

MAGIC IN THE SENSE OF something "inciting wonder" is here to stay; or if it is not, man will be vastly diminished by its loss. One need not be standing silent upon a peak in Darien. There is magic in the crash of surf on an unknown shore, but there is also magic in a mud puddle. There is a powerful magic in a crash of thunder, even more powerful in a nuclear explosion; but there is a very special magic in a child's kite or in the call of a gull and all that it evokes. Mark that leaf blown before the wind: it is important. No matter how sophisticated or blasé we become, that moment, this experience is all the treasure we shall reap in our few moments of identity.

What can rival a twilit meadow rich with the essence of June and spangled with fireflies? Here is magic, indeed, and the joy of pursuing through grass just touched with early dew a light now here, now there, now gone. Or of collecting several in a bottle and taking them indoors for illumination; or of tying one lightly with a thread to one's clothing, as natives of some tropical countries are reported to do at fiesta time. As children, we used to call them lightning bugs; in English-speaking countries, wingless kinds that emit a steady light from the ground are called glowworms. In fact, fireflies are neither flies nor bugs nor worms, but soft-bodied beetles called Lampyridae, a name based on an old Greek word that also evolved into our word "lamp."

Some of our commonest Lampyridae, curiously, give no light at all; these are day-flying beetles that one often finds on tree trunks, looking very much like ordinary fireflies but lacking the whitish "lamps" in their tails. The common European glowworm is a wingless female that produces a steady light, while the male of the same species is winged and not luminescent. Most fireflies of eastern North America are winged, and produce a flashing light in both sexes. The larvae (and even the eggs!) of many fireflies also glow. This seems strange when we consider that the lights of fireflies are used by the adults to find the opposite sex of their own species in the dark. What function does luminescence serve in the eggs and larvae? One might assume that the immature stages simply "can't help glowing," since the rudiments of the light organs are developing within them. But the fact is that the larval and adult organs are of quite different nature, and if the larval light-producing cells are carefully excised, the adult will still develop normal light organs.

Luminescence probably first arose as a dim and diffuse product of certain normal body processes, for many substances oxidized slowly in the dark produce a glow, and a dim luminescence occurs in many simple organisms (especially in the sea). Natural light is known to occur in certain bacteria, fungi, one-celled animals, sponges, jelly-fish–like animals, corals, marine worms, clams, snails, squids, arthropods, and of course a variety of deep-sea fishes—but never among the reptiles, birds, or mammals. It is possible that the earliest organisms on earth lived in an atmosphere devoid of oxygen. When oxygen first appeared—from the effects of sunlight on water vapor or from photosynthesis by primitive plants—it may have been toxic to these organisms. Luminescence may have developed as a system of getting rid of oxygen by burning it off as a "cold light." Later on, when plants and animals evolved that took advantage of oxygen to run their own body machinery, luminescence was preserved in a wide variety of organisms simply as a hangover from these ancient times. At least such is the belief of William McElroy and Howard Seliger, of Johns Hopkins University, our current leading authorities in this field. Their theory is supported by the fact that in many simple organisms luminescence seems to serve no function, and in some cases a single species exists in both luminous and non-luminous forms, both apparently successful. They also point out that luminescence requires oxygen in only very low concentrations, as it must have once occurred on earth. Certain bacteria, for example, produce light when the oxygen concentration is as low as one part in 100 million.

Obviously, some of the more complex animals—fish and insects, for instance—have elaborated this primitive light-producing capacity into specialized organs serving important functions in their lives. Adult fireflies possess the most complex light organs known, and these organs are still far from fully understood. Despite the intensity of the light they produce, the amount of heat is negligible. Only in very recent years have people developed chemical light-producing systems that rival that of the firefly in efficiency.

E. Newton Harvey, of Princeton University, has written a fascinating account of the history of human knowledge of luminescence. According to Professor Harvey, the firefly is not mentioned in the Bible, the Talmud, or the Koran, probably because fireflies are absent or uncommon in the arid regions of the Near East. However, the Chinese *Book of Odes*, dating from 1500 to 1000 B.C., speaks of the "fitful light of glowworms," and there are many accounts of fireflies in ancient writings of the Far East. The Japanese believed fireflies to be transformed from decaying grasses, while glowworms were said to arise from bamboo roots. In Japan, firefly collecting was popular in early times, and there is said to have been a firefly festival each year near Kyoto.

Aristotle was familiar with fireflies, and was apparently aware that some glowworms are the larvae of winged fireflies. The Roman encyclopedist Pliny believed that fireflies turned their lights off and on by opening and closing their wings, a statement repeated again and again down through the Middle Ages, along with a great deal of other misinformation, including tales of luminous birds. Thomas Mouffet (1553–1604) was aware that the British glowworms were females and that the males were nonluminous flying insects. Like many persons of his time, Mouffet was most interested in the medical uses of plants and animals. Fireflies, says Mouffet, "being drank in wine make the use of lust not only irksome but loathsome. ... It were worthily wisht therefore that the unclean sort of Letchers were with the frequent taking of these in Potion disabled, who spare neither wife, widow nor maid, but defile themselves with lust not fit to be mentioned."

The scientific study of insects is sometimes said to have begun with the publication of Ulysses Aldrovandi's *De Animalibus Insectis* in Bologna in 1602. Aldrovandi included a fairly accurate sketch of a glowworm, as well as the interesting hypothesis that fireflies use their lights to find their way about at night. A few years later Francis Bacon expressed curiosity that these insects were able to produce light without heat, but the times were scarcely ripe for a solution to this problem. The first important book on animal lights was written by the Danish physician Thomas Bartholin in 1647. Bartholin's own experiments failed when his glowworms escaped from the cage, but he discussed the unpublished work of Vintimillia, an Italian who observed the mating of fireflies in glass jars. Vintimillia was well aware that the flashes serve to attract the sexes, and he was the first to note that the eggs are luminous.

During the eighteenth and nineteenth centuries a great many persons turned their attention to the life histories and luminescent properties of fireflies, including such notables as Michael Faraday and Louis Pasteur. We nevertheless still have a long way to go; one can imagine a scientist of the year 2068 looking back to our time with somewhat the same amusement we now look back on Thomas Mouffet, although considering our increasing unmindfulness of the past, it is equally possible to imagine that in 2068 men will not look back at all.

Perhaps the most notable contribution to an understanding of the light of fireflies was made in 1885 by the French physiologist Raphael Dubois. Dubois removed a light organ of the beetle *Pyrophorus*, ground it up in water, and left it until the light went out of its own accord. He then removed another organ and ground it in boiling water for a short time, so that its light, too, was extinguished. Then he performed a neat bit of magic: when the two extracts were placed together, the light reappeared. He deduced that two substances were required to produce light, one of which was inactivated by heat. He called these two substances luciferin and luciferase (after Lucifer, who, among other more devilish traits, was the bearer of light). Dubois also learned how to obtain luminous bacteria from the skins of dead fish and squids on the seashore. The bacteria could then be transferred to culture plates, where they produced large colonies that glowed with a blue-green light. At the International Exposition in Paris in 1900, Dubois created a sensation by lighting a small room with flasks containing suspensions of these luminous bacteria.

A good deal more has now been learned about the production of animal light, and luciferin and luciferase have been obtained in purified crystalline form. McElroy and his colleagues at Johns Hopkins have synthesized luciferin. We now know that something more is needed: adenosine triphosphate (ATP). ATP may be less familiar to most persons than DDT or the CIA, but it happens to be even more important to us, providing as it does the energy for muscle contraction in animal bodies, including our own. In the light organ of the firefly, ATP energizes not muscles but the luciferin-luciferase system, the energy appearing not as mechanical work but as light. It has recently been proposed that luciferin and luciferase be employed in automated laboratories sent to Mars or other planets. The idea is that a scoop would pick up soil from the surface and mix it with water, oxygen, luciferin and luciferase. Then if a glow were televised back to earth, we would know that ATP, the fifth requirement for firefly light production, occurs there. The presence of ATP would mean, in turn, the existence of some kind of animal life in that alien soil. Thoughts such as these emphasize the need for caution when labeling the study of fireflies (or anything else) "useless" or "idle curiosity."

In the living insect, an additional element is needed to account for the working of the system: some sort of nervous control. It was discovered long ago that cutting off the firefly's head caused the flashing to cease, although in some cases the light organ glows dimly for a long time. Later it was found that by electrical stimulation of the severed nerve cord one can produce experimental flashing. It is believed that nervous control is centered in the brain; impulses then travel to the light organs via the nerve cord and via delicate nerves that closely parallel the minute tubes that carry air to the light cells. We still do not know exactly how the flash is triggered. Some have claimed that the nerves control the supply of oxygen to the light cells, but recent work suggests that the oxygen supply may be constant and that the series of chemical reactions resulting in a light flash may be initiated by the synaptic fluid of the nerve endings. That there are chemical intermediaries between nerve and light organ is suggested by the fact that a nervous shock provided directly to the light organ produces a very quick flash, whereas a stimulation to the nerves always involves a longer delay than nerve conduction itself would require. These are profound matters that we understand only poorly. Indeed, we still have much to learn as to how the chemical energy supplied by ATP is converted into the mechanical energy of ordinary muscle contraction.

The light organs of fireflies are complex structures, and recent studies using the electron microscope show them to be even more complex than once supposed. Each is composed of three layers: an outer "window," simply a transparent portion of the body wall; the light organ proper; and an inner layer of opaque, whitish cells filled with granules of uric acid, the so-called "reflector." The light organ proper contains large, slablike light cells, each of them filled with large granules and much smaller, dark granules, the latter tending to be concentrated around the numerous air tubes and nerves penetrating the light organ. These smaller granules were once assumed by some persons to be luminous bacteria, but we now know that they are mitochondria, the source of ATP and therefore of the energy of light production. The much larger granules that fill up most of the light cells are still of unknown function; perhaps they serve as the source of luciferin.

Actually, the light organs vary a good deal in different kinds of fireflies. We also know that the color of the light varies in different species and that this is a real difference in light color and not the result of a tinting or filtering effect of the window. Generally speaking, the light is yellowish, but it may have a greenish, bluish, or orange hue. McElroy has found that the color of the light produced by luciferin can be changed by altering the alkalinity of the solution, less alkalinity producing a shift toward the red end of the spectrum. Present evidence suggests that various species of fireflies have slightly different luciferase molecules, which cause the production of light of slightly different wave lengths. In the genus *Pyrophorus* (not really a true firefly, but a click beetle) there are two greenish lights just behind the head and an orange light on the abdomen. I well remember my first acquaintance with *Pyrophorus*. We were camped out near the ruins of Xochicalco, in Morelos, Mexico, when a disturbance caused me to peer out into the darkness: only to find that we were surrounded by pairs of

glowing green eyes. The ghosts of Toltec warriors a few yards
away? No, it proved to be a host of *Pyrophorus* in the bushes only
a foot or two away. The story is told that when Sir Robert Dudley
and Sir James Cavendish first landed in Cuba, they saw great
numbers of lights moving about in the woods. Supposing them to
be Spaniards with torches, ready to advance upon them, the
British withdrew to their ships and went on to settle Jamaica. In
this manner *Pyrophorus* may be said to have changed the course
of history.

The South American "railroad worm" is an elongate glowworm having eleven greenish lights down each side of the body
and two red lights on the head. These lights are quite brilliant,
and when the insect is moving along the ground it looks like nothing so much as a fully lighted railroad train. The North American
railroad worm is larger but lacks the red lights on the head. Both
of these insects are quite rare.

We now know that there are not only differences in the nature,
shape, and position of the light organs and in the color of the light
of fireflies but also (and most particularly) in the behavior patterns of the male and female during courtship and mating. The
males of the European glowworm fly toward a light only if it is of
the shape, color, and intensity of that of the female of that species.
In our common North American species, the females often rest
on the ground or vegetation, and flash only in response to the
flashes of the males. In one of the best-studied forms, *Photinus
pyralis*, the male flies near the ground in a strongly undulating
pattern; he approaches the bottom of one of these undulations
every six seconds, and as he does so he makes a half-second flash,
at the same time rising and thus describing a "J" of yellow-green
light. If he passes within a few feet of a female, the latter responds
with a half-second flash of her own, but only after an interval of
about two seconds (with only slight variation). This interval is an
all-important signal to the male; we know this because the male
will respond to various flashes, including even that of a flashlight,

but *only* when these occur about two seconds after his own flash. If the female flashes at the proper interval, he flies toward her and flashes again, whereupon the female again responds in two seconds. This may be repeated several times until the male reaches the female and mates with her. There is no evidence that sound or smell play any role in firefly mating.

The larger fireflies of eastern North America belong mostly to the genus *Photuris*, a confusing group in which the males show much variation in flash pattern but hardly any differences in structure or body color. For many years this problem bothered H. S. Barber, beetle specialist of the United States National Museum (not to be confused with H. G. Barber, a specialist on true bugs who worked at the National Museum at the same time—the two were "beetle Barber" and "bug Barber" to their colleagues). The results of H. S. Barber's study were not published until a year after his death in 1950. Barber found that in the Potomac Valley he could detect a woodland species with a short greenish-white flash once a second; a stream-side species with a slightly slower, faintly orange flash; a species occurring in alder groves and poising almost motionless, its light beginning dimly and glowing steadily in brilliance before stopping abruptly, only to reappear at a different point several seconds later; and so forth. Eventually Barber recognized eighteen species of *Photuris*, mainly on the basis of the flashes of the males; ten of these he had to name as new, since they had not previously been recognized. Needless to say, this did not endear him to museum workers, who could not very well sort their dead beetles on the basis of their flashes. But as Barber said:

"Taxonomy from old mummies which fill collections is a misguided concept. It leads to the misidentification of rotten old samples in collections. How these poor fireflies would resent being placed in such diverse company—among specimens of enemy species—if they were alive and intelligent! What contempt they would feel for the 'damned taxonomist.'"

Dr. James E. Lloyd, of the University of Florida, has recently completed a study of flash communication in the genus *Photinus*, the common smaller fireflies of the eastern United States. (Did you know that the Pacific coastal states, despite their many attractions, have almost no fireflies?) Lloyd, too, found several "hidden" species, first recognized by consistent differences in flash signals, and later found to differ in minor details of body color. In many places two or more species of *Photinus* fly together, but they are prevented from interbreeding by their different light signals. The males fly at different heights and in different flight patterns; their flashes differ in length, in the number of pulses per flash, and sometimes in the color or intensity of the light. The male is saying, in Lloyd's words: "Here I am in time and space, a sexually mature male of species X that is ready to mate. Over." The female of "species X" responds with a flash at the interval characteristic of her species—as described above for *Photinus pyralis*. Lloyd was interested in learning how much latitude was permissible without causing a "misunderstanding." In his experiments he used electronic devices for producing artificial flashes of known duration as well as for accurately measuring the response delay of the females. As in the case of all "cold-blooded" animals, things happen faster at higher temperatures, so in all his work temperature had to be taken into account.

In any given locality, the males and females are highly attuned to one another's messages; that is, the variation in responsiveness is such that they almost never answer another species. Females occasionally reply once to a flash of inappropriate length, but they do not continue to do so. On the other hand, if one compares the flash signals of species that do not occur together he often finds them to be very similar: here there is no possibility of mistakes being made, and refined "isolating mechanisms" have not evolved. It goes without saying that the integrity of species must be maintained, for interspecies hybrids are generally sterile (like the mule) or at least less well adapted for a specific role in nature.

One would assume that the larger fireflies of the genus *Photuris* (studied by Barber) always "speak a different language" from the small fireflies of the genus *Photinus* (studied by Lloyd). This is, of course, generally so, but with some fascinating exceptions. H. S. Barber commented on this as follows:

"Sometimes the familiar flashes of a small species of *Photinus* male are observed excitedly courting a female, supposedly of the same species, whose flashes appear normal to its kind, but when the electric light is thrown upon them one is startled to find the intended bride of the *Photinus* is a large and very alert female *Photuris* facing him with great interest. Does she lure him to serve as her repast? Very often a dim steady light near the ground proves under the flashlamp to be a small, recently killed *Photinus* being devoured by a nonluminous female *Photuris*. ..."

James Lloyd, while working on *Photinus*, found it possible to obtain females of a given species by walking about in a suitable habitat, imitating the flashes of the males with a flashlight. But now and then the females that signaled back to him turned out not to be *Photinus* females, but those of the genus *Photuris*, responding appropriately to specific signals of certain species of *Photinus*! Once he watched one of the *Photuris* females for half an hour and saw her respond to twelve passing *Photinus* males, in each case after the interval characteristic of that species of *Photinus*; all of these males were at least partially attracted to her. Finally a male landed near her, and after an exchange of signals ceased to light up after the usual time period. Lloyd checked and found that the *Photuris* female was clasping the *Photinus* male and chewing on him. As Lloyd points out:

"The answer to Barber's question has precipitated a deluge of new questions, not the least of which concerns the males of the genus *Photuris*. Is the female *Photuris* predaceous before she has mated? If so, how does her mate avoid the fate of attracted *Photinus* males? ... Can a single *Photuris* species prey upon more than one *Photinus* species with different signal systems? In other words, how many flash patterns do *Photuris* females have in the 'repertories,' and is predation on *Photinus* fireflies in any sense obligatory?"

It might be added parenthetically that insects are known that utilize luminescence not for courtship but strictly for luring and then feeding upon various small insects that are naturally attracted to light. Both in North America and in Europe there are certain gnat larvae that spin silken webs close to the ground and emit a dim, bluish light that probably serves to attract tiny midges and other insects into the web. An even better example is provided by the so-called New Zealand glowworm, which is not a true glowworm at all but another gnat larva. These insects live in certain caves in New Zealand and are so spectacular that guided tours are conducted into some of the caves. The gnats lay their eggs in a gluelike substance on the ceiling, and the larvae suspend themselves from silken sheaths and emit a bluish-green light that is said to lure small insects into the tangle of webs, where they are consumed by the larvae. F. W. Edwards describes the experience of entering the depths of one of these caves as follows:

"[After being warned by the guide to be quiet] we stepped cautiously in single file down, down to a still lower level. ... Then gradually we became aware that a vision was silently breaking on us ... a radiance became manifest which absorbed the whole faculty of observations—the radiance of such a massed body of glowworms as cannot be found anywhere else in the world, utterly incalculable as to numbers and merging their individual lights in a nirvana of pure sheen."

True fireflies are also capable of remarkable displays at times. Occasionally (especially in the tropics) untold thousands of fireflies will gather in a single tree or several neighboring trees and flash for many hours, sometimes for many nights in succession, producing a glow that can be seen half a mile or more away. Sometimes all fireflies in a tree have been seen to flash in synchrony.

Such displays have been reported from Southeast Asia and the East Indies for over two hundred years—but hardly ever from other parts of the world. Hugh M. Smith, while studying the fisheries of Thailand in the 1930's, often took parties of visitors down the Chao Phraya River near Bangkok to observe the displays. In an article in *Science*, he described them in these words:

"Imagine a tree thirty-five to forty feet high thickly covered with small ovate leaves, apparently with a firefly on every leaf and all the fireflies flashing in perfect unison at the rate of about three times in two seconds, the tree being in complete darkness between the flashes. ... Imagine a tenth of a mile of river front with an unbroken line of [mangrove] trees with fireflies on every leaf flashing in unison. ... Then, if one's imagination is sufficiently vivid, he may form some conception of this amazing spectacle."

Smith went on to say that the synchronous flashing occurs "hour after hour, night after night, for weeks or even months. ..." Reports such as Smith's have tended to remove much of the skepticism that greeted earlier accounts. (An author of an article in *Science* some years earlier had attributed the flashing to the twitching of the eyelids, remarking that "the insects had nothing whatever to do with it"!) For years the explanation of this unique phenomenon has intrigued John Buck, of the National Institutes of Health at Bethesda, Maryland, one of our leading authorities on fireflies. Some time ago he found that he could induce synchronous flashing on a small scale in the American firefly *Photinus pyralis* by using a flashlight at the usual interval of females of this species. When there were many males about, he could sometimes attract fifteen or twenty of them at once, and these would all adjust their flash periodicity in accordance with that of the female. "It is indeed an impressive sight," says Buck, "to see such a group converging through the air toward one point, each member poising, flashing and surging forward in short advances, all in the most perfect synchronism." It seemed possible that small groups such as this might build up within a larger aggregation and so stimulate one another that all fell into synchrony.

In another experiment, Dr. Buck placed a large number of males of this same species in a large, dimly lighted cage, where they soon began to flash in their usual manner. He then subjected the fireflies to sudden and complete darkness, whereupon all of them flashed at once, then again after four or five seconds. The synchrony persisted for some time and then disappeared. Buck felt that the unnatural advent of sudden, total darkness was not of importance in itself, but only because it served to increase the relative intensity of the flashes of neighboring fireflies, causing them to respond to one another's flashes as they would not ordinarily do in nature.

But of course these simple experiments performed on a North American species merely whetted his appetite for the real thing, and a couple of years later John and Elizabeth Buck took off for Thailand and Borneo. They were successful in finding "firefly trees," and they made photographs and photometric analyses that indicate synchrony of great numbers of individuals is indeed nearly perfect. They found that (contrary to earlier reports) both males and females occur in these trees, although the females do not participate in synchronous flashing. They showed that mating occurs in the trees, suggesting that the brilliant, synchronous flashes serve as a beacon to attract females from the surrounding forest. This may explain why this phenomenon is most prevalent along rivers in the Far East, for in this part of the world the exceedingly dense, tangled swamps would hardly be conducive to individual flash communication similar to that occurring in a New England meadow. But a "firefly tree" along a watercourse would provide an assembly beacon of ready access. Not only would the synchrony of the flashes increase the brightness but the alternation of light and dark would also be eye-catching, like the flashing neon signs that are a recent invention of man (though I would think that man has overdone a good thing, as he so often does).

The Bucks consider synchronous flashing to be a complex of behavior patterns (congregation, selection of certain trees, flashing, synchrony, and so forth) that have evolved together into a spectacular device for enhancing mating under otherwise difficult conditions. Evidently newly emerged males and females are constantly recruited from the surrounding forests, for individuals do not live more than a few days, and there must be a constant turnover in the population. The Bucks showed that males released in a darkroom are attracted to each other's light, and this suggests that wandering individuals might readily join a flashing swarm. It remains to be proved that there is a traffic of freshly emerged males and females into the trees and of mated females away from them. And it remains to be shown how the males maintain almost perfect synchrony from one end of a large aggregation to the other, when in fact laboratory studies suggest that the males react to one another over only short distances and that their reaction time is considerably greater than the variation in synchrony observed in nature. There is evidence that near-perfect synchrony occurs only in very dense aggregations, while in diffuse gatherings the flashing may be random. In some instances more than one species may aggregate in a given tree, resulting in a complex combination of flashes that is still presumably effective in attracting females of the species involved. All these are matters requiring much further study.

But of course scientists are used to partial and provisional answers; it is their stock in trade, and half the fun of science. H. S. Barber was well aware that his field studies of *Photuris* were only preliminary. And after a lengthy review of laboratory studies, John Buck concluded:

"In spite of the many morphological and physiological data which concern luminescence in the firefly, there seem to be surprisingly few unequivocal major conclusions which can be drawn."

This is "par for the course." Such is the complexity of living systems that tens of thousands of research workers all over the world each year push our knowledge forward by only a minuscule, with now and then a breakthrough that opens up a new area of ignorance. A century from now our great-grandchildren may marvel at how little we knew about fireflies. At least I hope so. In the meantime we may be unashamedly romantic or unflinchingly rigorous in our attitude toward fireflies, as befits our nature, and still know their magic.

8

Taxonomists' Curiosity
May Save the World

A few years ago I became dismayed by certain "leaders in thought" who claimed that only "important" species were worth studying (presumably they would decide which were "important"). Fortunately Smithsonian *was willing to provide me space to respond (1973) and later included the piece in* The Best of Smithsonian *(1981).*

IT WAS IN THE AUTUMN of 1728 that a young medical student with a passion for botany and a young divinity student with a passion for fishes met at the University of Uppsala—and the spark that leapt between them was to ignite a flame that is still burning. This was the age of enlightenment, the era of exploration—a time when the study of natural history had become respectable, and when expeditions to distant parts of the globe were reporting plants and animals previously undreamed of. What could be more important than to inventory all of the things of nature? But seven years later Peter Artedi, the divinity student, stumbled into a canal and was drowned, and it remained for Carl Linnaeus to bring their plans to fruition.

This he did with great success. His *Systema Naturae* went through 13 editions, each one something of a scientific best seller for its day. Furthermore, he set in motion what is often called "the Linnaean age," a long period when nothing seemed more worthwhile than to describe and classify species. Taxonomy—the science of classification—was a calling of the highest repute.

In retrospect, Linnaeus' system of naming organisms hardly seems revolutionary. Giving things double names—one a group (generic) name and the other specific—is as natural as speech itself. For example: red maple, grizzly bear, honey bee. Linnaeus used Latin, the scholarly language of his day, and very logically put the group names first: hence *Acer rubrum*, *Ursus horribilis* and *Apis mellifera*. It is true that Latin is no longer part of the education of most of us, but if Linnaeus had used his native Swedish, his system of names would hardly have become universal. And, as a dead language, Latin has no political connotations; to a Russian or a Japanese or anyone else, *Acer rubrum* is still *Acer rubrum*.

Such names can roll off the tongue like a song. I well remember how, as a college freshman, I delighted in surprising my friends with the name of the green sea urchin, *Strongylocentrotus dröbachiensis*. What a wonderful name! The cold fact is that those who find Linnaean nomenclature cumbersome have yet to propose a successful alternative. To a considerable extent, we are still in the Linnaean age, for we still use his system of binomial nomenclature; and taxonomists, by and large, are still committed to the belief that a complete systematic inventory of living things is not only possible but a matter of high priority. Nevertheless, both Linnaean nomenclature and the hope and need for a total inventory of nature are now being seriously questioned.

Linnaeus, in his *Species Plantarum* (1753) recorded about 7,300 species of plants, and in the tenth edition of *Systema Naturae* (1758) some 4,200 species of animals. But today the number of described species of flowering plants exceeds 300,000, and slightly more than a million kinds of animals are known. Many Linnaean genera are now regarded as families, and a host of new categories have been devised to accommodate all of these names. Classification has become so complex that textbooks can present only the barest outline (and hardly any two agree). The detailed classification of specific groups is often known to but a handful of people scattered widely about the globe—and they are unlikely to agree on all particulars.

In a recent article in *Science*, Peter H. Raven, Brent Berlin and Dennis E. Breedlove stated that there are approximately ten million kinds of organisms, and despite more than two centuries of effort we have still described only 15 percent of them. Furthermore, "the rapid growth of the human population will cause most of the remainder to disappear from the earth before they are seen by a taxonomist." So much for the dreams of Linnaeus and Artedi.

"The complete description of life on earth ... is impossible," wrote Paul Ehrlich of Stanford University almost ten years ago. And, more recently, Ernst Mayr of Harvard, one of the most widely respected figures in the field of systematics, expressed his opinion that "we need work in alpha taxonomy [that is, species] only in areas where such knowledge is essential." Unfortunately, he provides no rigid standards for deciding what is essential, and I suspect that the average businessman, congressman or (for that matter) college administrator would, on this basis, sweep all of taxonomy into the wastebasket.

I doubt that scientific progress has ever resulted from pursuit of the "essential." Rather, it has emanated from persons who were, above all, *curious.* And to accept any of the dicta quoted above is to say that to be curious about the diversity of nature is to be misguided. As R. J. Herrnstein of Harvard University has pointed out, "what looks 'important' at any time reflects a consensus based on what is already known." If this is true (as it surely is), one could make a strong case for the deliberate pursuit of what seems unimportant and nonessential (as I would).

A year or two ago I became interested in an obscure group of South American spider wasps of unknown relationships. I was puzzled because no females had ever been discovered, although males of several species were not uncommon in the collections of several museums. All of these males were banded with yellow and brown like many of the social wasps of the tropics, which are abundant and armed with powerful stings. After careful study of museum material and discussions with people who had collected these wasps in the field, I concluded that the females must have been placed in a different genus because, in overall form and coloration, they were utterly unlike the males. All had, in fact, blue-black bodies and orange wings, and were evidently mimics of tarantula hawks and other widespread wasps of similar color.

This proved to be the first known case of what I called dual mimicry; that is, a case in which the females and males of the same species belonged to very different mimicry complexes. It happens that in these wasps the two sexes spend most of their time in different habitats. Under these conditions it evidently had survival value (vis-à-vis vertebrate predators) for each sex to adopt a color pattern like the most pernicious stinger in its habitat. Having drawn these conclusions, I re-examined several other puzzling groups and found several additional examples.

Now I would be the last to claim that this research was essential, but it was gratifying; it fitted a few "loose pieces" into place and it resulted in a hypothesis of at least limited application. By some standards, no doubt I should have junked my manuscript. Recycled, the paper might have provided the wrapper for a package of spaghetti or some other essential commodity. As it is, I have added to the glutting of our libraries simply to satisfy idle curiosity. But I wonder whether most of what we now know about our environment didn't come about in much the same way.

Fortunately, there are many people who still find living things so terribly exciting that they cannot leave them alone. We live on a planet where, through several billion years, vast numbers of distinctively different kinds of organisms have evolved from simple primordial molecules. The processes we can now deduce, though with some uncertainties, and the products we can study in nature and in the holdings of our museums. To thinking persons they provide a drama without parallel. We have spent billions of dollars to collect a few sterile rocks on the moon. Has the dead moon become more essential to us than the living earth?

I agree that as human populations continue to expand, the delicately balanced environments of more and more living things will be destroyed; we see this happening every day. That is all the more reason to make an all-out effort to describe the diversity of life, for without such an effort we shall simply never know. And a case can be made for our greater dependence on the things of nature as the human population approaches saturation. The sperm whale is approaching extinction, but we have learned that an obscure desert plant called the jojoba produces a liquid wax very similar in chemical properties to sperm oil. We hear that a little-known beetle produces cortexone, a medically important drug, in amounts equivalent to the adrenal glands of 1,300 cattle. How can we know what organisms may enrich our lives—or permit us to survive a bit longer—if we cease to inquire? How can we be sure that we are not, this year, bringing about the extinction of a species that we may desperately need 50 years hence?

At the moment much research is being conducted on prostaglandins, very potent hormones that occur in minute quantities in most animal tissues and exhibit a startling array of pharmacological properties. Among other things, they appear to mediate inflammation, and a better understanding of their precise role may some day lead to more effective treatment of such persistent maladies as asthma and arthritis. A few years ago it was found that compounds closely related to prostaglandins occur in quantity in a gorgonian (soft coral) inhabiting West Indian reefs. The very limited supply of mammalian prostaglandin is expected to be supplemented soon by large quantities obtained by synthesis from precursor compounds in the gorgonian. This is exciting news for researchers and for pharmaceutical companies, one of which is already planning to harvest the reefs—one hopes with appropriate caution and good sense.

Paul D. Hurd, Jr., at one time chairman of the Entomology Department of the Smithsonian Institution, along with several coworkers, studied the systematics and host relationships of bees of the genus *Peponapis*. These bees collect pollen only from the blossoms of *Cucurbita*, a genus that includes our cultivated squashes and pumpkins, and there is evidence that the bees and their host plants evolved together in warmer parts of the Western hemisphere.

Not only has the systematics of the bees provided clues as to how cultivated squashes may have evolved from wild ancestors, but it appears that it may be possible to increase the yield of these crops in the Old World (where they were brought from America long ago, without bees) by establishing species of *Peponapis* in suitable habitats. Hurd and a coworker have described about a third of the species of *Peponapis*, and it is quite possible that the groundwork they have laid may prove far more relevant in retrospect than it ever did at the time.

Examples such as this could be supplied ad infinitum. In 1885 Carlos Berg, in the course of his studies of the Argentinian insect fauna, described a small moth as *Cactoblastis cactorum*. Did he foresee that 40 years later 60 million acres of Australian countryside would be overrun by alien cacti and that of 150 cactus-feeding insects surveyed, *Cactoblastis* would prove the key to the problem—nearly wiping out the cactus in a few years? Of course he didn't.

Could anyone have predicted the current search for "wonder drugs" in diverse and often poorly studied parts of the plant world? The discovery in recent years of antibiotics, muscle relaxants, hypo- and hypertensive agents, cortisone precursors and a startling array of hallucinogens had led Richard E. Schultes of Harvard to remark that "the Plant Kingdom represents a virtually untapped reservoir of new chemical compounds, many extraordinarily biodynamic, some providing novel bases on which the synthetic chemist may build even more structures." Professor Schultes cites an estimate that perhaps a fourth of the vascular plants of the New World tropics—a proven source of new drugs—

have yet to be described, and many of the described species remain poorly known. Is it appropriate to throw up our hands in despair, when we can be quite sure that discoveries of many kinds await those who work toward them?

Every blueprint for survival on Earth includes the substitution of biological control methods for chemical pesticides. Why is this proving so difficult? Because the parasitic wasps and flies that we wish to rely upon are so poorly understood. These are very tiny insects, requiring detailed study of their structures, life histories and host relationships. A good friend of mine who has devoted many years to the study of ichneumon wasps, perhaps the largest of all groups of parasites of pest species, had his research funds cut off, doubtless by persons convinced that we can "no longer afford" to be curious.

The opinion that taxonomists should discriminate species "only where such knowledge is essential" is hardly novel. One of my favorite quotes to taxonomy classes is the following: "It seems to me sufficient to consider those kinds [of organisms] which prove to us that they deserve to be distinguished. ... It seems to me that the many hundreds and hundreds of species of gnats and very small moths ... may be left confounded with one another."

This is from the Introduction of Réaumur's *Mémoires pour servir à l'histoire des insectes*, published in 1734, one year before the appearance of the first edition of Linnaeus' *Systema Naturae*. Are we to return to pre-Linnaean times simply because the task proved far more difficult than supposed?

I would like to reconsider, too, the statement mentioned earlier that we have only described some 15 percent of the ten million kinds of organisms. It is commonly agreed that most species of birds have been described, and a high percentage of the species of mammals, butterflies and several other "popular" groups. In the group I know best, the Aculeate wasps, I would estimate that more than 90 percent of the species north of Mexico have been described (though admittedly the tropics do not fare so well).

Speaking of the insect fauna of Australia—one of the most inadequately studied groups from one of the less well known continents—K. H. L. Key estimates that the description and naming of species may be 70 percent complete (although I think this percentage is a bit too high). Flowering plants continue to be described at the rate of about 3,700 species a year, but here (as in many groups) there is a certain amount of "overdescribing"—that is, the creation of unnecessary names in regional studies when more comprehensive monographs would demonstrate that several supposed species are one and the same. Of course, it is as much the function of good taxonomy to point out such synonymies as it is to discover novelties.

It is true that there are vast groups in which many thousands of species remain unrecognized, groups such as the nematodes, mites and parasitic wasps—ironically, groups showing much host-specificity and of potentially great importance to agriculture. This is depressing enough, or challenging enough, depending on one's mood. But it is not a cause for alarm. The task can and should be accomplished. Given the cost of only one moon shot, a great deal could be done in a few years, at least in a preliminary way.

Of course, no one pretends that to describe and name a species is to "know" it. This is only the first step to knowledge, but it is an essential step, not only because one needs to have a name for it, but because by placing it in a family and genus of organisms, one has the basis for predicting many things about it. This in itself serves as a guide to acquiring further knowledge. For example, I am currently describing a new wasp from Peru, placing it in the family Pompilidae (all members of which prey upon spiders and use one spider per nest-cell, so far as known) and in the genus *Aporus* (known species of which prey on trapdoor spiders and have structural modifications associated with this behavior). Thus something has been grasped in the realm of the unknown and placed in a position where more can readily be learned about it—one knows where to look and, in gross terms, what to look for. Such a matter might be critically important in medicine and agriculture; and no one can predict to what use such knowledge might be put in elucidating the structure of an ecosystem or in demonstrating some principle of evolution or animal behavior.

Members of a genus share certain common features of structure and biology, just as the genera comprising a family have fundamental similarities. A sound classification has enormous information content. Although the many categories recognized by the modern systematist may seem ponderous to the layman, in fact they reflect in remarkably concise fashion a vast body of sophisticated data. For Linnaeus, five categories sufficed. Such is our knowledge of living and fossil members of some groups that we now use more than 20 categories, from kingdom down to subspecies. The non-specialist may use as much or as little of this as suits his purpose. He may feel confident that if the classification is sound, it will lead him to almost any information he might require.

In the words of George G. Simpson, systematics "gathers together, utilizes, summarizes, and implements everything that is known about animals [and plants], whether morphological, physiological, or ecological." Our system of organizing this knowledge may not be perfect—but what is?

The time is long past when taxonomists contented themselves with the gross features of dead museum specimens. They are studying organisms in all stages of their life cycle; they are revealing minute, wholly unexpected structural details by the use of scanning electron microscopy; they are analyzing behavior patterns, chromosome configurations, and even the sequence of amino acids in protein and nucleic acid molecules.

Modern classifications reflect these approaches. This is cause for alarm in some taxonomic quarters, as what seemed to be one species has sometimes proved to be several. By analyzing song patterns, B. B. Fulton and R. D. Alexander have demonstrated that "the" field cricket of eastern North America is in reality seven species; although they could not be differentiated on the basis of dead specimens, they fail to interbreed in nature. Studies of egg color and structure, along with other biological features, revealed that "the" malaria mosquito of Europe was actually six species, only two of which actually transmit malaria effectively. Use of a minute parasitic wasp to control the California red-scale insect, a serious pest of citrus, led to inconsistent results until Paul DeBach and his colleagues discovered that what was thought to be one was actually seven different species, each having its own biological characteristics. This discovery provided a vastly improved basis for control and permitted the introduction of several new species of scale-insect parasites.

Such discoveries are exciting and of fundamental importance. We still pay homage to Linnaeus, but we have gone very far beyond the brief Latin descriptions of superficial features that sufficed for his day.

It is ironic that in our time, when ecology has truly become a household word, young systematists are having even more difficulty than usual in finding positions. In the words of Edward O. Wilson, writing in the journal *Ecology*: "Most of the central problems of ecology can be solved only by reference to details of organic diversity. Even the most cursory ecosystem analyses have to be based on sound taxonomy. ... The food nets, the fluctuation of population numbers ... the colonization of empty habitats ... and most other basic topics of ecology, require a deep understanding of the biology of individual taxa." Yet there are large groups of organisms having only one or two specialists in the entire world, and sometimes none at all.

"It is the exclusive property of man to contemplate and to reason on the great book of nature. She gradually unfolds herself to him who, with patience and perseverance, will search into her mysteries." As a person caught in the turmoil and surfeit of our times, I have become blasé about a great many things and a doubter of many human enterprises and supposed values. But I have never questioned the sentiments expressed by Linnaeus in the above sentences from the introduction to his *Systema Naturae*.

I am not sure whether, at this stage, a more profound knowledge of the biosphere—including, as a first step, an inventory of living things—would save us from destroying the Earth as a viable habitat for man. Perhaps not. But it would be nice to think that we tried at least to acquaint ourselves with the cast of that greatest of all dramas that began with a primordial soup and one day yielded a superb green world filled with remarkable creatures, including, at least for a few ticks of the cosmic clock, a being that imagined himself master of the Earth.

9

The Natural History of Flies

I have written a good many book reviews through the years, but most were of ephemeral interest and not worth repeating. However, I tend to be "carried away" by flies (and doubtless soon will be, literally, by their maggots). So I include a somewhat condensed version of my review of Harold Oldroyd's book The Natural History of Flies, *which was published in* Scientific American *in 1966.*

THE NOUN "FLY" has three separate meanings. Originally it meant any flying insect, and as such it has become the basis of many vernacular insect names: dragonfly, mayfly, ichneumon fly, and the like. Students of insects find the word useful only when it is applied to a coherent group—the order Diptera, defined as a group of insects exhibiting complete metamorphosis and possessing as adults a single pair of wings. (Actually flies have a second pair of wings, but they are modified to form a pair of halteres, or balancers.) To most people a fly is a housefly or any of several similar species found in and around human habitations. One can forgive the nonspecialist who is confused when he is told that a firefly is not a fly but a mosquito is (although in fact the word "mosquito" is merely a diminutive of *mosca*, the Spanish word for fly). Here we have a familiar dilemma in science: should a word in common use be abandoned because it is imprecise, or should it be defined more precisely and the public educated to accept the definition? Scientists almost always choose the second alternative, and therein lies a major source of misunderstanding between the scientist and the nonscientist.

Harold Oldroyd, senior dipterist at the British Museum (Natural History), has probably had more flies cross his desk than anyone else in the world. This may seem a dubious distinction to some, but readers of the readable and attractive book Oldroyd has produced are likely to conclude that it is, after all, a rare and exciting privilege. The book is particularly recommended for those who so eagerly study the photographs of the surface of Mars for signs of life. There may not be much of anything on Mars, but on the earth there are some 80,000 species of flies, many of them little known and most of them a good deal stranger than the organisms that fill the dreams of exobiologists.

Have you heard, for example, of the downlooker fly, which sits head down on the trunk of a tree "as if it were looking for a victim"—when in fact no one knows what it feeds on? Or of the coffin fly, which maintains itself through many generations on human bodies buried in coffins, although no one knows how it gets into them? Or of the petroleum fly, known only from pools of crude petroleum in California, where it lives on other insects that become trapped in the oil? Or of mosquitoes of the genus *Malaya*, which subsist by filching honeydew from the jaws of worker ants? There is hardly a page in Oldroyd's book that does not introduce the reader to one fantastic fly or another, and hardly a paragraph that does not contain a confession of ignorance and an implicit plea for more studies on the life histories of these ubiquitous but little-understood animals.

In his introduction Oldroyd admits that a book such as his may easily degenerate into "a series of anecdotes of the 'wonders' of fly-life" unless it has a theme. Oldroyd's theme is the evolution of flies, and his approach is a comparative one. The flies are seen as representing two evolutionary lines. One comprises the crane flies and various groups of midges, gnats, and mosquitoes. The other consists of the "flies proper," which for the most part possess more robust bodies and shorter antennae, and culminate in the house-fly, the bluebottle fly, and others less well known to most people.

Oldroyd's summaries of recent research on flies, as well as his bibliography, will be found particularly useful. His anecdotes en-liven the text, perhaps not always in quite the way intended. We read, for example, of the housewife who pricked some sausages in the frying pan and saw maggots pop out of the holes—the con-sequence of a sausage-making machine not being thoroughly cleaned. We read also that "Professor G. C. Varley [of Oxford] told me that he himself had been bitten in California by *Symphoromyia sackeni.*" To bite Californians is one thing, but to bite Professor Varley—tsk, tsk.

One of Oldroyd's pet themes is that adult flies, "where neces-sary, make up for the deficiencies of the larva;" that is, when the larval diet is deficient in protein, the adult is likely to be a blood-sucker, but when the larva is carnivorous, the adult is likely to concentrate on carbohydrates. Oldroyd cites many examples, none better than the mosquito *Megarhinus*, which has carnivorous larvae but adults that feed on flowers, in strong contrast to other mosquitoes. Still, there seem to be many exceptions. For exam-ple, both the larvae and the adults of most of the larger horseflies are carnivorous, and the plant-feeding larvae of gall midges most certainly do not give rise to bloodsucking adults. Since one of the major selective advantages of complete metamorphosis is that it enables the insect to exploit quite different habitats at different stages of its life, one should expect many cases in which the food habits of the larvae and adults differ. We know much too little, however, about the nutritional requirements of the majority of flies to indulge in such broad generalizations.

Perhaps the most striking aspect of the evolution of flies is sim-ply that this originally rather heterogeneous array of gnats and midges gave rise to something of a "utility model"—a fly of rather standardized appearance developing from maggots and pupae of decidedly standardized appearance, yet physiologically *capable de tout.* Most of the higher flies seem "stamped in the same mold;" the consistent displacement of a few bristles may result in their being assigned to different superfamilies by taxonomists. The development of such a "standard type" of animal, apparently incapable of much further morphological improvement but capable of rapid evolution in physiological features (as indicated, for example, by the development of strains of houseflies resistant to certain insecticides), represents a challenge to biologists and perhaps to all mankind. One cannot help thinking of the first individualistic automobiles and comparing them with modern mass-produced models, all of which look very much alike.

Indeed, the term "mass production" fits the flies quite well. The housefly, one of the most complex miniaturized systems in existence, is able to produce a new generation of its kind in less than a week. It has been calculated that in the course of a single summer a pair of flies could produce enough offspring, if all survived, to cover the earth to a depth of 47 feet. Oldroyd checked these calculations and found "that a layer of such a thickness would cover only an area the size of Germany, but that is still a lot of flies."

All of this is cause for concern when one considers that the housefly habitually breeds in human feces and then travels to human foods and feeds by first regurgitating onto them, and that other flies are capable of burrowing under man's skin or developing in his intestines. I rather wish Oldroyd had quoted from the accounts of people who have described the sensation of *Dermatobia* larvae burrowing in their skin, or of individuals suffering from intestinal or nasopharyngeal myiasis.

The reader is doubtless thinking that this sort of thing could never happen in the blacktopped, air-conditioned world of today. Malaria, yellow fever, filariasis, sleeping sickness—fly-borne diseases that once swayed empires—have all become minor diseases; the apple maggot and cheese skipper have been banished from the A&P. Farmers nonetheless pay several million dollars a year to control crop-infesting flies, and local outbreaks of encephalitis, a mosquito-borne disease with a high rate of mortality, are reported in the U.S. every summer. We learn from E. C. Cushing, quoted by Oldroyd, that during World War II the U.S. armed forces employed 4,407 men for antimalarial work in the South Pacific alone; in spite of this the Army had 546,230 cases of malaria. Can we afford to let down our guard against the flies? Can we ever have confidence that a catastrophe in human affairs will not force us to lower our guard?

Man has been pestered by flies ever since the dawn of civilization, and doubtless before. In Harry Eltringham's words,

> *Profound research does not disclose*
> *The epoch when the fly arose*
> *To plague creation.*

The Philistines made obeisance to Beelzebub, the god of flies, in the hope of propitiating him and so reducing the curse of flies. Malcolm Burr, in *The Insect Legion: The Significance of the Insignificant* (1939), speaks of this as "the first historical account of the appointment of a Fly Control Officer." Then came the 10 plagues of Egypt, six of which (according to Burr) were entomological, and at least two and perhaps four of which were attributable to flies. Fly-borne diseases are said to have hastened the decline of both Athens and Rome. Sleeping sickness long delayed the civilizing of Africa and yellow fever the opening of the American Tropics.

These stories have been told many times before. What of the future? Oldroyd believes that with luck and persistence we may be able to keep most bloodsucking flies under control. The higher flies may have better prospects: "They have learned to use decaying, fermenting, or putrefying organic materials, universal media that will always exist. No doubt we shall continue to campaign against the housefly, but we shall not defeat it by chemicals, because it evolves resistant strains too quickly for us. Hygiene will keep it at bay in superior districts, but there will always be plenty of breeding material left about for it. As quickly as urban areas are denied to the housefly the tourist and his motor-car make more rural areas attractive to it."

If human populations (and their wastes) are to double every few generations as predicted, there may be a rich future in store for the filth flies. Perhaps we had better learn to understand and appreciate them. Vincent G. Dethier, in his delightful book *To Know a Fly* (1962), makes a strong case for the blowfly. As for me, I hope to seek out the coffin fly. By the time he finds me, it will be too late to enjoy him.

The possibility that we are already becoming more fly-conscious is suggested by the recent publication of *A Catalog of the Diptera of America North of Mexico*. This catalog is the work of a devoted band of dipterists in the Entomology Research Division of the U.S. Department of Agriculture, assisted by more than 40 collaborators, each of them a specialist on some particular group of flies. Like many other entomologists, I shall be eternally grateful to them for completing such a tedious and thankless task. Why, indeed, should it be thankless? I hereby thank the 47 dipterists listed in the catalog, not 1,000 times, but 16,130 times—the number of species of flies they record from America north of Mexico.

Under group after group in the catalog one finds such comments as "many vexing taxonomic problems remain unresolved" and "very little is known of the habits or immature stages." Let us hope that publication of this catalog ushers in a new era in the study of Diptera. When we consider the many ways in which flies impinge upon us, and the remarkable life histories of so many of them, it is not much of a tribute to our intellect that while reaching for the stars we ignore the fly on our windowpane.

10

Enjoying Insects in the Home Garden

Some years ago the Smithsonian Institution Press asked me to write a book about insects as part of a series they were doing. When it arrived it turned out to be a little different than the Press had anticipated, so it was published sui generis, *in paperback, in 1985. It was titled* The Pleasures of Entomology: Portraits of Insects and the People Who Study Them. *It was (like all my books) fun to write. Here is the better part of one chapter.*

THE GROWING OF VEGETABLES in one's backyard has much to recommend it. Some thirty-eight million Americans have such gardens, altogether occupying nearly two million acres. The flavor and food value of freshly picked vegetables so far exceed those of the store-bought equivalent that gardeners look forward eagerly to each year's harvest—and spend cold winter days planning next year's. (I always order my seeds from the catalog on the day the IRS forms arrive; it takes away some of the pain.)

It is claimed that despite the high cost of food these days, one doesn't really save money by having a home garden—if one counts the cost of one's own labor. But who wants to count that when gardening is such good exercise and so full of challenges and rewards? What will the summer's weather be like? Drought? Hail? Early frost? Will we have enough sweet corn to invite friends for a corn roast? How many canning jars will be needed?

Then, of course, there are insects to think about. Will flea
beetles be abundant this year? Will leaf miners decimate the beet
greens? Will the cabbage butterflies find the broccoli? (Of course,
they always do.) Shall I ring the garden with marigolds to keep
the grasshoppers out? (Doesn't work; they love marigolds.) Shall
I sacrifice my ideals and stock up on insecticides? Or shall I plant
a little more than we need and simply enjoy the insects, the rabbits, the birds?

There is much to be said for the last suggestion. Our garden is
not far outside our picture windows, and as we drink our coffee
we can watch the robins and grackles slipping into our strawberry
patch and emerging with their beaks smeared with red. Now and
then a squirrel stares into the patch, then dives in, emerges with
a berry, and takes off for the nearest tree. Like the rabbits that
nibble the peas, he has learned that we may pursue him. It is fun
for all; of course we never catch anything.

Each year I look forward to the insect inhabitants of the garden.
I don't begrudge them their share; they amuse us, inform us, and
often stimulate our sense of beauty. If they take what I consider
more than their share (a fairly rare event) I don't mind being a bit
brutal. No animal should multiply so as to destroy its environment (though, being a member of the species *Homo sapiens*, I may
have no right to say that).

As I write this I am rearing some zebra caterpillars that were
skeletonizing the leaves of our roses. (We do make space for
flowers, which after all are food for the spirit.) The zebra cater-
pillar is very beautiful indeed: its head is orange, its body yellow,
with three pairs of black, longitudinal stripes, each pair separated
by a white streak. In color it rivals the orioles that are nesting in
our cottonwoods. One does, of course, need a microscope to fully
appreciate the beauty of zebra caterpillars, but that is an essential
item in the household of everyone who admires insects. The
caterpillars don't remind me much of zebras. I prefer the scientific name, *Ceramica picta*, which I would translate from the Greek
and Latin to mean "a painted earthen vessel."

It has been a good year for asparagus beetles. I am glad; we had a good harvest, and the beetles are most decorative on the bushy flowering stalks. There are two kinds, and we have them both. One, officially called *the* asparagus beetle, has a black head, antennae and legs, with an orange collar and blue-black wing covers bordered with orange and bearing six light yellow spots—as elaborate a color pattern as one could design. The other, called the spotted asparagus beetle, is wholly orange except for black "polka dots" on its wing covers. The two kinds have similar defensive behavior; if the bush is shaken they simply release their grip and drop to the ground, a response called "thanatosis" in the scientific literature, where suggestive terms such as "playing dead" are frowned upon. If captured, both emit high-pitched squeaks, presumably addressed to birds and other predators, which may drop them in surprise.

Neither species feeds on anything other than asparagus, and hardly anything else in the insect world will eat asparagus. Is there some chemical in the plant that repels herbivores? How does it happen that two related species of beetles can live together on the same plant at the same time—a seeming contradiction to the rule that complete competitors cannot coexist? What is the significance of the fact that the eggs of the asparagus beetle are laid in rows in an erect position, while those of the spotted asparagus beetle are laid singly, flat against the stems? How did two related species happen to evolve such brilliant and such different color patterns?

It appears that the larvae of the asparagus beetle feed freely on the foliage, while those of its spotted cousin live primarily within the seeds. Thus to a certain extent they share the plants and are not complete competitors. Perhaps, with some research, I could answer the other questions. But these are difficult questions, without simple answers. And there are so many other unanswered problems within a few yards of our back door!

To consider only the question of food specialization: we have plenty of "finicky eaters," gourmets, if you like: asparagus beetles,

Mexican bean beetles, tomato hornworms, and others. We also have plenty of insects that will eat almost anything: cutworms and grasshoppers, especially. It is intriguing to speculate on the advantages of being a specialist, when the disadvantages are so obvious. Clearly, if I don't plant beans, I won't have bean beetles, and if nobody plants them (and there are no wild ones) the bean beetles will become extinct. Specialist feeders are closely linked to their hosts and must suffer when the host declines, just as the chestnut weevil disappeared when the chestnuts vanished from eastern forests as a result of the blight.

Yet there are clear advantages in being a specialist, for specialists have of necessity evolved responses to specific cues of their host plants (usually chemical) and use these cues to find their favored plants readily among the myriad of plants in nature and in gardens. Often the plants they specialize on have repellent or even poisonous chemicals. Volatile mustard oils in members of the cabbage family, for example, repel many insects, but enable cabbage butterflies to zero in on plants on which their larvae thrive. An alkaloid called tomatine, in tomatoes, is toxic to many leaf-feeders, but hornworms have evolved digestive systems that get rid of the toxins without suffering any ill effects. By having overcome certain repellent or toxic substances, host-specific insects have the plants pretty much to themselves, without serious competition. Quite often they make use of the toxins to render themselves distasteful to predators. This is what the milkweed bug and the monarch butterfly have done with the cardiac glycosides of milkweeds. Perhaps that is the explanation of the predominantly orange coloration of asparagus beetles, orange being the "warning color" of many distasteful insects.

In contrast to specialist feeders, generalists can find food almost anywhere and will often eat weeds and wild plants as well as garden plants. But they tend to avoid or do poorly on plants containing toxins or repellents, since they haven't developed the ability to overcome the specific chemicals of defended plants—

and it would hardly be possible to evolve mechanisms for over-coming such a diversity of chemicals. Even in bad grasshopper years, tomatoes remain inviolate.

Of course there is no such thing as a "complete generalist;" even gypsy moths don't eat everything in sight. And there are few that confine their feeding to a single species of plant, although there are many that feed on a few related plants, usually members of the same family. Cabbageworms (the larvae of white cabbage butterflies), for example, feed readily on cabbage, broccoli, brussel sprouts, and cauliflower—all members of the cabbage family having similar leaf chemistry. Parsleyworms (the larvae of black swallowtail butterflies) feed on carrot tops, parsley, dill, and parsnips, all members of the carrot family (Umbelliferae).

Parsleyworms are most welcome denizens of our garden. They are elegant creatures, transversely banded with green and black and ringed with orange spots. When disturbed, they erect a pair of orange "horns," actually eversible glands that secrete a repellent substance that smells like rancid butter—in fact it is butyric acid, the essence of rancid butter. It is an enjoyable experience to collect the mature larvae or chrysalids and rear the butterflies indoors, where one can follow the expansion of their glossy, spangled wings. We always release them outdoors, of course, where they can find mates and plants on which to lay their eggs. Their larvae are seldom abundant; it would take a lot of them, all season, to do as much damage to our carrots as the local rabbits can do in one evening.

Parsleyworms are fastidious feeders, requiring food containing certain essential oils, such as methyl chavicol, which is found principally in members of the parsley family. They will even attempt to eat paper if it is soaked in these oils. On members of the parsley family, they can feed without serious competition from other insects, since parsleyworms have evolved the ability to thrive in the presence of psoralens, substances that deter feeding by most other insects by binding DNA in the presence of ultraviolet light.

G. Wayne Ivie and his colleagues in the U.S. Department of Agriculture have recently fed tissues treated with carbon-14–labeled psoralens to fall armyworms (which are very general feeders) and to parsleyworms. They found that parsleyworms rapidly detoxify the poisons in their midgut, so that they do not enter the body fluids to any great extent; within 1.5 hours, 50 percent of the carbon-14 passes out with the feces. By contrast, fall armyworms accumulate more psoralens in the body tissues, and within 1.5 hours only 1 percent of the carbon-14 has appeared in the feces. So it is not surprising that, despite the appetite of armyworms for plants of many kinds, they do not flourish on parsley and related plants.

It is interesting that some members of the parsley and carrot family are relatively unpalatable to parsleyworms. Paul Feeny and his colleagues at Cornell University have shown that cow parsnip and angelica have evolved certain modifications of the form of the psoralen molecule that cause a reduction of the growth rate and fecundity of parsleyworms. They cite this as an example of coevolution: parsleyworms first evolved a means of overcoming the effects of psoralens, in members of the carrot family, and later certain members of this family evolved a modification of the molecule that parsleyworms could not handle. Will parsleyworms further evolve the ability to overcome this novel plant defense? In a few hundred years, perhaps a few thousand, the answer should be apparent.

On the other hand, some plants of the parsley family that grow as wildflowers in woodlands lack psoralens, which are ineffective as deterrents in the absence of plenty of light. Unlike most umbellifers, these plants are attacked by a variety of generalist feeders.

Parsleyworms, cabbageworms, and similar insects were the subject of a 1964 article that has become something of a classic of entomology: "Butterflies and Plants: a Study of Coevolution." The authors were Paul Ehrlich, of Stanford University, and Peter Raven, of the Missouri Botanical Garden. The science of plant-insect relationships has since blossomed into a major field, the subject of several books and innumerable scientific articles. Once these relationships are better understood, it may be possible to breed varieties of crop plants that either lack the chemical cues re-quired by pest species or that have repellent or toxic properties with respect to these species. ...

That, incidentally, is one of the strongest reasons for preserving as much of the wild plant world as possible: the genetic material needed for the breeding of resistant stocks may lie in wild relatives of wheat, corn, and other crops. The rapid extinction of species and locally adapted populations that is occurring as a result of wide-spread habitat destruction is not pleasant to contemplate as we look forward to feeding the crowded world of the future.

Many of the seeds available to home gardeners are, in fact, those of varieties that have been developed for resistance to vari-ous diseases and insects. However, neither our basic knowledge of this complex subject nor our technology has advanced to the point that we need fear that next year we will miss the cabbage-worms, the parsleyworms, the asparagus beetles, and all the other insects that provide half the joy of gardening.

The growing of potatoes in the home garden is not especially practicable, but I often plant a few simply because I like to have a few Colorado potato beetles around. There are few insects that have played so prominent a role in the history of entomology. The Colorado potato beetle (often called simply "the potato bug") is our gift to Europe—a recompense, so to speak, for their gift of the asparagus beetle, the Hessian fly, the cabbageworm, the gypsy moth, and so many others. According to Reece Sailer, of the Uni-versity of Florida, more than 1,300 "foreign" insects have become established in the forty-eight contiguous states, some 800 of these deserving to be called "pests." But the Colorado potato beetle is a native of Mexico and the southwestern United States that has spread over most of North America and much of Europe, pro-ducing a wave of devastation of one of humankind's most basic crops, the potato.

Pioneer entomologist Thomas Say first discovered the potato beetle in 1824. He found it "on the upper Missouri," and although he did not record the host plant, we now know that the beetles originally fed on a common western weed known as buffalo bur (*Solanum rostratum*). It was not until the early settlers brought the potato to the West that this once obscure insect ran rampant.

Potato (*Solanum tuberosum*) is a close relative of buffalo bur, with similar leaf chemistry, and the beetles found it thoroughly palatable. They spread from one potato patch to another, often destroying the whole crop. By 1864 they had reached Illinois, where state entomologist Benjamin Dann Walsh remarked that they marched through the state "in many separate columns, just as Sherman marched to the sea." By 1874 they had reached the Atlantic coast— a remarkably rapid spread for a relatively weak-flying insect, suggesting that some had "hopped a train east."

But we should not pass up Walsh so briefly. He was a colorful person, who went about the fields in a long cloak and a tall, cork-lined hat. When he caught an interesting specimen he impaled it on a pin and attached it to the cork lining of his hat. Late in life, while walking down a railroad track reading his mail, he was overtaken by a train and injured in such a way that he had to have a foot amputated. He looked forward to having it replaced with a cork foot, he told his wife, so that "when I am hunting bugs in the woods I can make an excellent pincushion out of it."

Walsh had been a classmate of Charles Darwin, and like Darwin had collected insects as a youth. But after he moved to Illinois, in 1838, he became a farmer and lumber merchant. When he was fifty he retired to devote himself to entomology. Although he lived only another dozen years, he published 385 articles on insects and coedited, with Missouri entomologist C. V. Riley, a short-lived, semipopular journal, *American Entomologist.* He was appointed Illinois' first state entomologist, and in this capacity made a careful study of what he called "the new potato bug."

Walsh had little use for those who tried to sell farmers quick remedies for every pest. The Union Fertilizer Company (whose

secretary was appropriately named A. S. Quackenbosh) advertised a substance that it claimed was "sure death and extermina-
tion to the Cankerworm, the Curculio, the Apple Moth, the
Potato Bug ... and all descriptions of insect. ..." Walsh replied:
"The trouble with all such panaceas ... is that we hear nothing of
the ninety and nine cases where the [remedy] was applied and
found to do no good. ... Nothing is more certain than that there
is no Royal Road to destruction of the Bad Bugs; and the only
way in which we can fight them satisfactorily, is by carefully
studying out the habits of each species. ..."

Walsh followed his own advice, studying the biology of a number of important insects. But he by no means confined himself to
"pest" species and their "control;" he made pioneering contributions to systematics and to ecology and evolution. He wrote of
the restrictions of insects to certain host plants and the possibility
that species might evolve after continued breeding on a particular host. This was in 1868, not long after the publication of *The
Origin of Species* and decades before plant-insect relationships became a major theme in entomology.

But to return to the Colorado potato beetle, after still another
diversion. So serious a threat was it during the last few decades of
the nineteenth century that there was a desperate search for effective controls. Since (like asparagus beetles) these insects "play
dead" when disturbed, one recommendation was to jar the plants
so that the beetles would fall into a pan of kerosene or onto the
ground, where, on a hot day, they might perish from the heat.
Chemical insecticides were in a primitive state in the 1860s, and
the first widespread use of chemicals to control insects is associated
with the need to contain this pest. The arsenic-containing pigments
Paris green and London purple were used at first, but later replaced by lead or calcium arsenate. Arsenicals came to be used
for many insects, although nowadays they have for the most part
been replaced by other substances. Incidentally, the first wide-
scale test of the effectiveness of DDT, in 1941 in Switzerland, was
against the Colorado potato beetle. Today one hears less about the

beetle, as its natural enemies have to some extent caught up with it, and potato growers have established procedures for ridding themselves of this pest and several other insects and diseases.

It was in 1921 that the beetles became established in France. By 1935 they had reached Germany, and by the 1970s they were raising havoc as far east as Russia and Turkey. One of mankind's most staple foods was in jeopardy, and research proliferated in Europe as it had in the United States. More is now known about feeding behavior of these beetles than that of perhaps any other insect.

One of the first persons to study the matter was Professor C. T. Brues of Harvard University, whose 1946 book *Insect Dietary* was an early effort to summarize knowledge of this intriguing subject. Brues kept twenty-four of the potato family (Solanaceae) in his greenhouse and found that some provided acceptable food for Colorado potato beetles and some did not. Oddly, the adult beetles seemed attracted to tomatoes (which are also Solanaceae), although their larvae did not thrive on them. Brues called this "an extreme case of mistaken instinct." It now seems not surprising, since we know that tomato leaves contain a toxic alkaloid, tomatine. The native home of the tomato was quite different from that of buffalo bur, the original host of the potato beetle. Consequently, the beetles never evolved, as part of their genetically programmed behavior, the ability to discriminate between the leaf odors of their true host and those of a related plant that was toxic to them. Colorado potato beetles are also attracted to ornamental petunias, which like tomatoes are native to South America, but these solanaceous plants are also unsuitable as food for the larvae. When larvae are forced to feed on petunias, they vomit and become more or less paralyzed.

Ting H. Hsiao, of Utah State University, and Gottfried Fraenkel, of the University of Illinois, showed in 1968 that adult Colorado potato beetles, when given a choice, show a slight preference for laying their eggs on buffalo bur, as compared to potato, and a strong preference for laying their eggs on deadly nightshade (which belongs to the same genus as potato, *Solanum*). But deadly nightshade does not support larval growth at all. Hsiao and Fraenkel found that for egg-laying females, the physical nature of the leaves does not matter; they will lay eggs on hairy or spiny leaves, or even on glassware or paper towels, provided they receive the proper volatile chemical stimulation. ...

Hsiao and Fraenkel, in the laboratory, tested Colorado potato beetle larvae on 104 species of plants of 39 families. They found that 80 percent of them were rejected by the larvae, presumably because they contain feeding inhibitors or toxins. But surprisingly, the larvae accept and grow well on certain nonsolanaceous plants such as milkweed and lettuce. However, these plants lack the necessary attractants for the adult beetles, so they are not accepted in nature. Obviously, host-finding and feeding are controlled by quite different factors—probably true of many host-specific insects. This is a "fail-safe" way of insuring that all goes well. But of course a modern garden contains plants that had their origins in many different parts of the world. Here they are crowded together and surrounded by a variety of weeds of even more diverse origins. Rather than accusing insects of occasional "mistaken instincts," one can but admire their ability to thrive in the midst of such a diverse and alien environment.

So there is something to be said for the Colorado potato beetle as a paragon of successful gourmandizing. The prison-striped adults and the sluggish, corpulent larvae have found a place in the history of entomology and in the development of research both on ways of killing insects and on ways of understanding plant-insect relationships. Despite all this attention, the beetles are still there, waiting to infest our potatoes, joining the cabbageworms, the parsleyworms, the hornworms, the cutworms, the bean beetles, the asparagus beetles, and all the others—so that everyone may enjoy a miniature zoo in his backyard.

11

To the Ant, and Beyond, with Edward O. Wilson

Orion published this profile in their summer issue, 1986. Wilson has since published his highly acclaimed autobiography, Naturalist *(Island Press, 1994). Much of what I said in 1986 is described more fully in* Naturalist, *but my own perspective on this unusual person may still be worth preserving.*

ANTS ARE NOT THE MOST ADMIRED of animals. They are too inclined to invade our kitchens, to crawl up our legs when we are trying to relax in the sun, to spoil good agricultural land with piles of soil they defend with fiery stings. But myrmecologists— scientific students of ants—hold them in the highest esteem, as paragons of the successful exploitation of diverse environments and the ultimate exemplars of social living.

Whatever one's opinion of them, ants cannot be ignored. One estimate has it that there may be 10^{15} ants on earth—that is, something like one quadrillion. A single colony of one of the African driver ants may contain twenty million individuals. But one need not go to the tropics to appreciate fully the abundance of ants: the acre and a half of the Colorado Rockies that I call home is occupied by two people and many tens of thousands of ants. One colony of thatching ants has built a nest five feet in length and two feet high, all neatly covered with twigs and pine needles; I should hate to have to count the ants in it. (Can we call it *our* property when we are so grossly outnumbered?)

Ants are decidedly mind-boggling. And not just in terms of their numbers. As Lewis Thomas puts it in *The Lives of a Cell,* "Ants are so much like human beings as to be an embarrassment. They farm fungi, raise aphids as livestock, launch armies into wars, use chemical sprays to alarm and confuse enemies, capture slaves. ... They exchange information ceaselessly. They do everything but watch television." It is not surprising that students of ants are often inspired to expand their vision well beyond the objects of their study and to find in the societies of these remarkable animals fresh insights into the world we live in. Auguste Forel, following publication of his youthful monograph, *The Ants of Switzerland* (1874), became a psychiatrist, a social reformer, and director of a hospital for the insane. Erick Wasmann, a Jesuit scholar who lived in the Netherlands, made a great many valuable studies of ants and their parasites and associates, seeing in them manifestations of divine powers. The American myrmecologist William Morton Wheeler, author of the classic (but now badly out-of-date) book *Ants: Their Structure, Development, and Behavior* (1910), wrote and lectured on sociology, education, and diverse other subjects. The title of a posthumous collection of his writings, *Essays in Philosophical Biology,* suggests the breadth of his thinking.

On the contemporary scene, Edward Osborne Wilson is one who has been inspired by his studies of ants to look with a keen eye at many facets of life, particularly human nature and the human-nature interface. "There are no lessons to be taken home from the direct observation of colonial life in the insects," he writes. But "they offer us an entrée into a much deeper analysis of social evolution." A bold and original thinker and a facile writer, Wilson has had a career marked by a good deal of controversy, but one that has gained him election to the National Academy of Sciences while still in his thirties, profiles in leading magazines, guest lectureships in this country and abroad, six honorary degrees, and the National Medal of Science. In spite of such heady honors—perhaps partly because of them—he always returns to the ants, the wellsprings of his intellect.

I first met Ed Wilson in the zoology lab at the University of Alabama, where I was visiting a former fellow graduate student from Cornell. A young man was in the laboratory messing with ants; he was skinny, slightly hard of hearing, and partly blind in one eye—hardly someone to be taken seriously, I thought. I had seen far too many students whose early enthusiasms had been squelched by society's indifference. Here was a person easily so squelched and unlikely to compete successfully in the rigorous world of science. How wrong I was! In a few years this young man had gone on to Harvard as a graduate student, and he later ascended that university's academic ladder to an endowed professorship. For a time he and I were colleagues there, and though I have long since departed from those hallowed if sometimes fractious halls, I still devour his writings—to date, ten books and over 250 journal articles. I continue to envy his elegant style, laden as it is with uncommon ideas and with literary allusions new to me.

Wilson was born in 1929 to an old Alabama family, the only child of a couple who separated while he was quite young. His father worked for the Rural Electrification Administration and traveled widely in the South. Ed attended sixteen different schools in eleven years—not a formula for developing childhood friendships. Though he grew up something of a loner who was most at home in the local woods and fields, he often acquired a companion whom he "turned into a part-time zoologist" (his words, in a recent autobiographical sketch from which I shall often quote). By his relatives he was "thought to be a little strange but smart, and he was expected to make something of himself; what, nobody could quite figure out, but *something.*"

In his recent book *Biophilia,* Wilson lovingly describes some of the country he roamed in Alabama and the Florida Panhandle, as well as some of the folklore of the region.

"It is a wonderful thing to grow up in southern towns where animal fables are taken half seriously, breathing into the adolescent
mind a sense of the unknown and the possibility that something
extraordinary might be found within a day's walk of where you
live. ... I found my way out of Mobile, Pensacola, and Brewton to
explore the surrounding woods and swamps in a languorous
mood. I formed the habit of quietude and concentration into
which I still pass my mind during field excursions, having learned
to summon the old emotions as part of the naturalist's technique."

Wilson's love affair with ants began in Washington, D.C.,
where he lived for some time when he was ten years old. He
spent many hours at the Smithsonian Institution and the National
Zoo—and at Rock Creek Park, the closest approximation to the
woodlands he knew in the South. In the park he discovered a
colony of lemon ants, small yellow ants that produce an odor of
citronella. About the same time he read an article on ants by
William Mann, director of the zoo. Mann had been a student of
W. M. Wheeler at Harvard and had explored the Amazon Basin
and other remote areas for ants. These were exciting prospects for
a budding myrmecologist.

Back in Alabama, Wilson began a study of the ants of that state
and made his first important discovery (at the age of thirteen):
that a new and better adapted form of a fire ant species native to
South America was well established in the Mobile area. In 1949,
while a senior at the University of Alabama, he was hired by the
state department of conservation to make a detailed study of the
imported fire ant. Several important publications resulted. At
Harvard Wilson would go on to discover, in 1959, the gland that
produces the chemical used by the ants to lay odor trails to
sources of food—the first of his many contributions to the field of
animal communication. Fire ants are tiny, hardly an eighth of an
inch in length, and it took very careful dissection to isolate several
organs barely visible to the naked eye. When he strung out the
contents of one of these structures, called Dufour's gland, near a

nest, "worker ants poured out of the nest by the dozens, ran the length of the artificial trail, and milled about in confusion at its end." From beginnings such as this, the study of chemical releasers (pheromones) has blossomed into a major discipline in biology. The trail pheromone of the fire ant and other pheromones have since been identified and synthesized, and some have been used in the monitoring or control of pest insects. .

By the late fifties, Wilson was well launched on other tracks in his multifaceted career. As a graduate student at Harvard he had been awarded a grant to work in New Guinea and elsewhere in the South Pacific.

"For ten months, from November 1954 to September 1955, I worked in Fiji, New Caledonia, the New Hebrides, New Guinea, Australia, and Sri Lanka. On the way home I visited the leading ant collections of Europe to include taxonomic research. I had experienced the great expedition at last: New Guinea was Rock Creek Park writ large.

"Every young evolutionary biologist should have such a *Wanderjahr*. ... It provides a source of information and ideas on which years of creative work can be built, and a lifetime of memories."

At Harvard, Wilson not only had access to the largest ant collection in North America, but he also established a lasting friendship with another "ant fanatic," William L. Brown, Jr., whom he calls "the single greatest influence on my scientific life." Together they spent many hours in what Wilson called "megathought," tackling in their youthful enthusiasm a number of problems in biology that others had shied away from—or had thought were already solved.

Wilson's work during his twenties and thirties included major contributions to systematics, behavior, ecology, and biogeography—many of them charting new paths in their fields. What was the secret of so great achievement? His originality he attributes to his handicaps: because of poor vision in one eye, he has unusually keen vision in the good one, and a supposed learning disability gave him a tendency to "reconstruct much of what I learn, often with new images and ways of phrasing." As for his productivity: "I have always been a workaholic." I can add to this that he is the most self-disciplined person I have ever known. Rising early, he jogs or walks for a time, then repairs to his laboratory, where he works until noon. After a bag lunch, he works for a few more hours before returning to his family (he was married in 1955, and he and his wife have a daughter). Evenings are spent reading, not only science but poetry, philosophy, and, for relaxation, mystery stories.

Except when doing field work, he still follows much of this regimen. Of course, in Academia one must always make time for meetings with graduate students, colleagues, and visitors. Also, he has taught a course in general biology, using a text he coauthored, as well as an advanced course in evolutionary biology. In addition he is curator of Harvard's extensive insect collection.

He has never been one to waste a minute that might be spent in research or writing. Confronted by a major task, he becomes completely immersed in his work. When he was writing *Sociobiology*, he explains, "for two years I averaged ninety hours of work a week in order to complete the book while meeting my duties at Harvard." He has been fortunate in having a devoted secretary who for twenty years has helped him with library work and manuscript preparation. When he feels inadequate to a task he has set out for himself, he goes about acquiring the necessary skills. From time to time he has taken courses at Harvard, in mathematics and philosophy, for example.

All of this may make it seem that Wilson is more a machine than a person, which is far from the case. With friends, he is the warmest of people, sparkling with lively conversation and good humor. When we were both at Harvard, my wife and I wrote a biography of W. M. Wheeler, completing it while we were on sabbatical leave in Australia. From time to time a letter would arrive, written in a shaky handwriting and signed by Professor

Wheeler (then dead many years). "Wheeler" asked irately why we had not sent him specimens of *Nothomyrmecia*, the world's most primitive ant (which had not been found for many years, though it was later rediscovered by Wilson's former student R. W. Taylor). Of course the letters were from Ed Wilson.

During his graduate student days, Wilson took a long field trip with Thomas Eisner, another insect enthusiast, now a professor at Cornell University. Eisner remembers that while they were driving across a particularly uninteresting part of the Great Plains, Wilson remarked to the effect that "one of these days someone will have to produce a synthesis of everything that has been done on the social relations of organisms." The thought germinated in Wilson's mind for some years. In the 1960s he began to put together a comprehensive review of knowledge not only of ants but of all social insects, including the termites, social bees, and social wasps. The result was *The Insect Societies* (1971), the first book of its kind for many years and the first to consider social insects from the point of view of modern population biology. *The Insect Societies* was favorably reviewed in *Science, The New York Times,* and elsewhere. I have found it such a valuable source of information that *both* my copies are decidedly the worse for wear.

Wilson did not rest on his laurels, but proceeded to expand upon his theme. A final chapter of *The Insect Societies* was entitled "The Prospects for a Unified Sociobiology." In it he wrote:

"As my own studies have advanced, I have been increasingly impressed with the functional similarities between insect and vertebrate societies and less so with the structural differences that seem, at first glance, to constitute such an immense gulf between them. ... The formulation of a theory of sociobiology offers one of the great manageable tasks of biology for the next twenty or so years."

Sociobiology: The New Synthesis was published in 1975, only four years after *The Insect Societies,* and like it received enthusiastic reviews. This was a lavishly illustrated tome of 698 oversized pages, monumental both in its size and in its implications. The societies of animals from the lower colonial invertebrates (such as the Portuguese man-of-war) through the social insects to vertebrates (including humans) were reviewed, in the search for the general theory that he had proposed as a major task of biology. As in the case of *The Insect Societies*, Wilson consulted many researchers in putting together so much information, and all the chapters were reviewed by specialists on those topics. The introductory sentences of his final chapter alone, on human sociobiology, were enough to raise the hackles of many academics who were comfortable in their traditional disciplines.

"Let us now consider man in the free spirit of natural history, as though we were zoologists from another planet completing a catalog of social species on Earth. In this macroscopic view the humanities and social sciences shrink to specialized branches of biology; history, biography, and fiction are the research protocols of human ethology; and anthropology and sociology together constitute the sociobiology of a single primate species."

A few months later, Wilson published a popular account of some of these ideas in *The New York Times Magazine*. It was titled "Human Decency is Animal" and was illustrated with several of Sarah Landry's beautifully executed drawings from *Sociobiology*. The theme was that altruism—self-sacrifice for the benefit of others—is widespread among animals. Worker ants forgo sex, and labor for the colony; honeybees die in defense of the hive; dolphins lift stricken individuals to the surface so they can breathe; chimpanzees share food and care for orphans. The explanation for this behavior, and a key element in sociobiology, is kin selection. Briefly, an individual may achieve reproductive success not only through his own efforts, but through others who share many of his genes; everything depends on the extent of the sacrifice and the degree of relationship.

The usefulness of the concept of kin selection is nowhere more apparent than in trying to understand the enigmas of social life among ants and other social insects. Most individuals in an ant (or honeybee) colony are sterile, and thus have no direct way to transmit their genes to future generations. But all colony members carry similar genes, and it is the interaction of environmental factors with these genes that causes individuals to develop into members of one of several castes. Workers and soldiers spend their lives helping to rear other individuals, a few of whom are specialists in reproduction. In this way, despite their personal sterility, via their kin they do transmit their genes, and more effectively than they could if they themselves mated and laid eggs.

So it is quite possible for seemingly disadvantageous traits such as sterility, or any sacrifice that diminishes an individual's personal success, to be favored by natural selection if they benefit closely related individuals. The cost to the donor must, of course, be balanced again the benefit to the receiver. The British biologist J. B. S. Haldane pointed this out, facetiously, some years ago when he said that he would lay down his life for two brothers or eight cousins—since brothers on the average share half their genes and cousins one-eighth.

Can acts of human heroism and self-sacrifice be thought of in these terms, or are they "transcendental qualities that distinguish humans from animals?" Wilson proposed no firm answer, but suggested that the question is by no means off limits to biologists. Perhaps, he said, even homosexuality may have evolved in an early period of human evolution to provide a partly sterile worker caste; if a society of "interrelated homosexuals and heterosexuals regularly left more descendants than similar groups of pure heterosexuals, the capacity for homosexual development would remain prominent in the population as a whole." (There is considerable evidence that homosexuality does have a genetic basis; it may not be advantageous in our modern welfare society, but from this perspective it is by no means perverted or degrading.) Ideas such as this—and the ultimate conclusion that all unselfishness is really selfish—needless to say were not easy for everyone

to swallow. Even less so were the suggestions that many aspects
of human social behavior—even matters of ethics—might have a
genetic basis.

That Wilson had thoroughly and admirably portrayed the elements of social behavior in lower animals was undeniable. But
applied to humans, was it a rehash of old ideas on nature versus
nurture; or was it a real breakthrough—and if the latter, was it a
breakthrough that was likely to benefit human society? Wilson's
style was deliberately provocative, and the response was swift.
Within a year, University of Chicago anthropologist Marshall
Sahlins was out with a book titled *The Use and Abuse of Biology: An
Anthropological Critique of Sociobiology*. It was apparent that some
anthropologists, at least, had little understanding of the field of
evolutionary biology—and felt that Wilson had insufficient grasp
of their own field. Many psychologists were equally skeptical,
committed as they were to explaining behavior in terms of responses to the environment.

But these exchanges were gentlemanly and to be expected as
a result of Wilson's forceful and polished presentation of a point
of view that to many seemed novel as well as threatening to established beliefs. Science progresses by such interactions. What
Wilson did not anticipate was outspoken opposition on political
rather than scientific grounds, much of it based among his colleagues at Harvard. A Marxist-oriented group called Science for
the People attacked sociobiology in several leading journals as
"biological determinism," meaning that if much human behavior
is genetically determined, such things as racism, sexism, and class
warfare are justifiable. Incited by these distortions of sociobiology, members of another group began to picket and at times actually disrupt Wilson's lectures—no matter what he happened to
be discussing. Matters took a nasty turn at the 1978 meeting of
the American Association for the Advancement of Science, when
a member of this group leaped to the stage and poured water on
Wilson's head. What these people seemed to be saying was that

the study of the genetic basis of human behavior was not the province of science, that in fact limits should be set on inquiry when it threatened fixed ideologies.

Wilson characterized the situation as follows:

"The issue at hand is vigilantism: the judgment of a work of science according to whether it conforms to the political convictions of the judges, who are self-appointed. ... I am ideologically indifferent to the degree of determinism in human behavior. If human beings proved infinitely malleable ... then one could justify any social or economic arrangement according to his personal value system. If on the other hand, human beings proved completely fixed, then the status quo could be justified as unavoidable.

"Few reasonable persons take the first extreme position and none the second. On the basis of objective evidence the truth appears to lie somewhere in between, closer to the environmentalist than to the genetic pole."

The popular press made much of the controversy. In an article titled "Shockley Revisited," *Newsweek* reported that some of Wilson's critics had placed him in the same category as William Shockley, a Stanford physicist who has had much to say about the genetic basis of race and of intelligence. The cover of *Time*, August 1, 1977, was splashed with the headline "Why You Do What You Do." Despite the catchy and misleading headline, *Time*'s article was on the whole sympathetic to Wilson and to other adherents of sociobiology. Similarly, there was a profile of Wilson in *Discover* in 1982; it was well done, but the editors could not resist the title "It's All in the Genes."

In 1978 Wilson published *On Human Nature*, addressed to a wider audience than his previous books and largely successful in reaching that more general readership. For it he received the Pulitzer Prize for nonfiction in 1979. He argued eloquently that all forms of mental activity and social behavior—including aggression, sex roles, ethics, and even religion—can be more meaningfully understood against a biological background. That is, of course, not the same as saying "It's all in the genes." Reviewers pointed out that many of Wilson's ideas lacked rigorous proof. Others, like myself, found the book tremendously thought-provoking—and I am sure that is exactly what the author intended.

By this time Wilson was, in his words, "battle fatigued from the controversy over human behavior and wanted to draw more completely back into research on social insects." But a young physicist from the University of Toronto, Charles Lumsden, proposed that he and Wilson explore more deeply the linkage between genetic and cultural evolution. Together they wrote *Genes, Mind, and Culture* (1981), an attempt to develop models for visualizing the coevolution of genes and culture. This book is decidedly tough going, and two years later the authors published a more popular account of their findings in a book called *Promethean Fire*. Members of Science for the People were outspoken in their criticism, but the authors defended their views well. In a round table discussion broadcast by the British Broadcasting Corporation, the moderator concluded that Lumsden and Wilson "had taken hold of an important and interesting problem, but ... a great deal remains to be done before [their theory of the coevolution of genes and culture] will be comprehensively established."

What, finally, can be said of sociobiology? My own library now has a full shelf of books on the subject, and several journals are either dedicated to the subject or consider it regularly. Many of these publications deal not with human behavior but with that of insects, mammals, and other social organisms, and there is no question but that as a result of Wilson's work, research in this field has flourished with a fuller appreciation of the importance of population structure, kin selection, and the richness of social communication. As for human behavior, many social scientists and students of the humanities are now discussing sociobiology openly and without invoking the ire of their colleagues. Indeed, new lines of communication have opened between disciplines that in the past have remained within their own tight little circles. Wilson himself has adopted a less provocative stance, remarking in 1978 that sociobiology "might at best explain a tiny fraction of human social behavior in a novel manner. Its full applicability will be settled only by a great deal more imaginative research by both evolutionary biologists and social scientists. In this sense the true, creative debate has just begun." Perhaps the day will yet come when the gap between what C. P. Snow called "the two cultures" will be bridged. [In 1998 Wilson made a valiant effort in his book *Consilience*.]

As a result of the controversies aroused and the publicity they received, it is likely that many persons link Wilson's name with sociobiology and only with that field. However, it is just one of several threads that have run through his productive career. During his youthful *Wanderjahr* in the South Pacific, he became intrigued by the relationships he observed between the number of species on islands, and the size of the islands and their distance from other land-masses. This led to a collaboration with Princeton ecologist Robert MacArthur on a landmark book, *The Theory of Island Biogeography* (1967). One of their major postulates was that island faunas tend to be in an equilibrium in which immigration and extinction of species are balanced against one another. To test this hypothesis, Wilson and his student Daniel Simberloff undertook to remove, by fumigation, all the insects and other arthropods on several small mangrove islands in the Florida Keys. It was a novel and ambitious undertaking.

On their first trip to southern Florida, Wilson and Simberloff arrived just as hurricane Alma was sweeping in from the Caribbean—a wonderful opportunity to study the effects of a hurricane on the fauna of mangroves. While more reasonable people were streaming inland, the two researchers hastily purchased some raingear—a couple of thin, plastic women's raincoats were all they could find—and headed for a coastal swamp. In a driving rain and winds that nearly blew them flat, they watched limbs being torn from the mangroves, ant colonies drowning in the waves, and lizards rafting on floating debris. They could not have asked for a better demonstration of how physical stresses influence isolated faunas! But after a while they became sufficiently wet, cold, and frightened to repair to a motel and wait out the storm.

The mangrove project involved frequent trips to selected small keys (each having only one or a few trees) and the hiring of a fumigator, as well as a crew to erect tents over the islands. Wilson reveled in steering his skiff through the shallow, treacherous waters, recalling that his Confederate great-grandfather, "Black Bill" Wilson, once smuggled guns past the blockade of Mobile before being captured and imprisoned by Admiral Farragut. Their work paid off: over time the defaunated islands were reoccupied by close to the original number of species—not always the same ones—establishing that the number of organisms an island can support is determined by its size and its distance from land-masses supplying its immigrants.

The close relationship of size and distance to diversity is an idea that can be applied not only to islands in the ocean but also to plots of forest, lakes, or any habitat surrounded by a different environment. These concepts are useful in planning nature preserves and in designing environments that allow for human expansion without unduly decimating the plants and animals. In 1978 Wilson was appointed to the Scientific Advisory Committee of the World Wildlife Fund, later to its Board of Directors.

The loss of organic diversity resulting from habitat destruction has been a major concern of his for many years. This is again a controversial topic—human expansion and development versus the preservation of the environment in which we evolved. In the broadest sense it is the same controversy; are we part of nature and subject to its laws, or are we something apart and able to flaunt those laws at will?

In a recent article in *Wilderness*, he spoke of species diversity as an ethical goal, taking his cue from pioneer ecologist Aldo Leopold, who proposed that all ethics rest upon the premise that the individual is a member of a community of interrelated parts—and a community with both a past and a future.

"Why then should the human race protect biological diversity? Let me count the ways. The first is that we are part of life on earth, share its history, and hence should hesitate before degrading and destroying it. The acceptance of this principle does not diminish humanity but raises the status of nonhuman creatures. We should at least pause and give reason before treating them as disposable matter."

Recognizing that people are more apt to conserve land and species if they see material gain in so doing, he went on to point out that presently we depend upon less than 1 percent of living species for our existence. But there are vast numbers of potentially useful plants and animals, many of them still to be discovered. Some provide new sources of food, while others have potential uses in medicine or industry. If one argues that people come first—an argument, surely, to be taken seriously—a strong case can still be made that extinction of species is an irretrievable loss to the human enterprise. Yet the present rate of species extinction is believed to be about one thousand per year, and the figure is expected to pass ten thousand a year—nearly a species a minute—within a few decades. A substantial portion of this loss will occur when tropical rain forests are finally reduced to a few isolated patches unable to sustain much diversity or to provide living space for larger animals.

Wilson's belief in the importance of the linkage between humans and the natural world provided the substance of his 1984 book, *Biophilia*, a very personal account of his explorations in nature and the joys of discovery, as he searched for ants and for an understanding of community living. "Biophilia" he defines as more than a love of nature, as an "urge to affiliate with other forms of life." But these other forms of life are slipping away from us as we expand our own populations and, of necessity, our agriculture and industry.

"I find it astonishing that so little attention is being given to the exploration of the living world. The set of disciplines collectively called evolutionary biology, including initial field surveys, taxonomy, ecology, biogeography, and comparative biochemistry, remains among the most poorly funded in science. The amount spent globally in 1980 on such research in the tropics, where the great majority of organisms live, was $30 million—somewhat less than the cost of two F-15 Eagle fighter-bombers, approximately 1 percent of the grants for health-related research in the United States, or a few weeks' liquor bill for the populace of New York City."

Wilson has proposed nothing less than a complete inventory of life on earth, to be accomplished through a revival of systematics, the study of biological diversity, a study that, in a recent editorial in *Science* magazine, he terms "a fountainhead of discoveries and new ideas in biology."

[In 1992, Wilson brought many of these ideas together in his book *The Diversity of Life*, beautifully illustrated and written with his usual eloquence. Meanwhile, in 1990, he and his colleague Bert Hölldobler had produced a monumental volume titled simply *The Ants*, which was awarded a Pulitzer Prize, Wilson's second.]

Each of Wilson's major paths of development began with the ants; they have led him to new insights into communication, into the structure of societies and of natural communities, into human nature, into the need to preserve at least some parts of the environment in which we evolved and which we still need. But of course ants were not merely a point of departure; they were in themselves the object of much fundamental research, still ongoing. When I last visited Ed Wilson, he gave me a tour of his laboratory. Thriving colonies of ants covered the shelves. With his usual intensity, he was delving into the systematics and behavior of one of the largest and most difficult genera.

Perhaps, I thought, if politicians and other movers and shakers of our society could be converted to myrmecology, we could all look to the future with greater optimism.

12

A Remarkable Bird, the Magpie

The tropics abound in elegant birds, and I treasure my brief acquaintance with mot-mots, manakins, and quetzals. In the summer months, a few brilliant tropical birds invade our climes: hummingbirds, tanagers, and others. But one very handsome bird, worthy of the tropics, is here year round, and I for one am willing to forgive its noisy ways and its appetite for road kills. This tribute was published in Colorado Outdoors, January-February 1988.

AS THE LEWIS AND CLARK EXPEDITION approached the upper reaches of the Missouri River in 1804, Meriwether Lewis noted "a remarkable bird (Magpy). ... About the size of a large pigeon, a butifull thing." The magpies flew into their tents and snatched food; during the skinning of game, they lurked about and dashed in to steal pieces of meat. Although new to Lewis and Clark, the birds had long raided Indian camps for offal from their hunts, and even accompanied buffalo hunters to share in their spoils. Indian boys sometimes kept them as pets.

The West has been vastly transformed since Lewis and Clark traversed plains and forests swarming with bison, elk, wolves, sage grouse and a great variety of other wildlife. The High Plains and Rocky Mountains, though proclaimed by Major Stephen Long in 1823 to be "almost wholly unfit to cultivate," proved a comfortable home for human-kind—though at the expense of much of the native fauna. Those that continued to flourish either were ignored as having little impact on the human enterprise, or were wily enough to avoid serious decimation of their populations. Magpies, I am glad to say, survive and flourish on both accounts.

Is there a more elegant bird? No half-way measures; no grays or pastels; deep black and pure white sharply defined, the black reflecting iridescent green in the sunlight. In flight, patches of white mark the short wings, and a great tail trails behind. No rapturous melodies issue from their throats, to be sure, but they do have an unusual variety of unmusical sounds that doubtless serve them well enough.

The huge bill is an efficient tool for handling a variety of carrion, insects, and vegetable matter. In the summer, grasshoppers, caterpillars, and maggots plucked from carrion and dung are the preferred diet. In winter, almost anything even remotely edible will do, including road kills and suet filched from bird feeders. Magpies occasionally land on the backs of cattle, deer, and other animals, where they pick off the ticks but sometimes pick at sores. From time to time they have been reported as killing sheep, behavior that has sometimes resulted in local campaigns against them. A newspaper in British Columbia, in 1931, reported the slaughter of over a thousand magpies. They are sometimes inadvertently killed when attracted to poison bait intended for coyotes. Over 5,000 magpies were killed in Oregon a few years ago in this way.

In North America, the magpie is strictly a western bird, and no bird is more characteristic of the West, whether it is gliding down a canyon, pecking at a carcass, or chattering in concert with others from a grove of cottonwoods. The range of the magpie extends from New Mexico to Alaska and on into Eurasia, in fact all the way to England. In Europe, magpies have become the stuff of folklore and superstition. One of the legends inspired an opera by Italian composer Gioacchino Rossini, *La Gazza Ladra* (The Thieving Magpie). Spanish artist Goya included a magpie in his portrait of Osorio de Zuniga, a tribute to mankind's long fascination with this magnificent bird.

More than 400 different names have been applied to the magpie. As for the word itself, some suppose that it is a contraction of "maggot pie," with reference to the birds' habit of picking maggots from flesh. Others claim it is compounded of the common French name Margot and the Latin word for woodpecker, pica. The latter word comprises the scientific name of the species, *Pica pica* (rather easier to remember than most scientific names). Ornithologists insist we call it the black-billed magpie, to distinguish it from the yellow-billed magpie of California.

Magpie nests consist of great piles of twigs, usually toward the tops of small trees. Often they measure about two feet in diameter, but when they are reused they may become considerably larger; one record nest measured seven feet from top to bottom. The base and sides are built of coarse sticks, often thorny ones (Russian olives are favorites when available). Inside there is a cup of mud, lined with rootlets and horsehair; over the top is a canopy of twigs. There is an opening on each side, one for entry and another to accommodate the long tail. As a general rule, magpies nest in small colonies and the nests are spaced out along a wooded valley or similar habitat. Nests are defended from intruders with noisy calls and aggressive displays. Intrusions by neighboring magpies sometimes result in savage fights.

Magpies mate for life, but it is said that lost mates are quickly replaced from a pool of unmatched individuals. They start nesting in March, the male bringing in most of the larger twigs, the female doing most of the lining. In April, the female lays 7 to 10 speckled eggs and incubates them, the male feeding her while she does so. When the nestlings hatch, in about 18 days, they are fed by both parents, primarily on insects that are caught on the ground. When young magpies are taken from the nest and hand-reared, they can sometimes be taught a few words. Like their cousins the crows, magpies are counted among the more intelligent of birds.

In his monograph on the magpie, Jean Myron Linsdale comments that "the general manner of a magpie is that of a bird well able to take care of itself." Good for the magpie; we live in times when wild creatures must adapt to our curious ways or join the ranks of endangered species. Magpies are inquisitive birds, but ready to take alarm when danger approaches. They have learned to live with people, but with caution. Surely their appetite for insects more than makes up for their infrequent transgressions. And surely Meriwether Lewis was right that a magpie is "a butifull thing." Hardy and adaptable, winging free over canyon and plain, it is one of the West's more accessible treasures.

13

The Cache la Poudre

When we moved to Colorado in 1973, we soon became enamored of our local river and spent many a day exploring the stream and its tributaries. In 1991 Mary Alice and I wrote a book about it: Cache la Poudre: The Natural History of a Rocky Mountain River *(University Press of Colorado). I include here an essay about one of our favorite tributaries as well as a section of our final chapter.*

Killpecker Creek

The three Balds—North, Middle, and South—barely break the treeline, at about 11,000 feet, but they are visible for many miles around and give rise to several streams: the east fork of Roaring Creek to the south, Elkhorn and Lone Pine Creeks to the east, and Killpecker to the north. Killpecker is the least of these, running a course of only a little over two miles from the slopes of North Bald to the North Fork of the Poudre. A good trail provides access to fine forests and the secrets they hold.

It is a rare treat, hiking in country that is not overly endowed with rain or snow, to come upon a series of springs. Those near the source of the Killpecker are especially generous, their waters issuing from the hillside in unexpected places and forming translucent pools among moss-covered rocks. Mayflies dance over the springs, as if to celebrate so delightful a break in a forest that is otherwise almost a monoculture of lodgepole pine. Arrow-leaved yellow ragworts and blue delphiniums tower over the springs two to three feet tall, capturing and seeming to magnify the sunlight that filters through the pines. Both seem more appropriate to a tropical rainforest than to these subalpine woodlands.

Ragwort seems an inadequate name for so radiant a plant. Fortunately there are some alternate names: butterweed, groundsel, squaw-weed. The genus is *Senecio*, based on the Latin word *senex*, meaning an old person and alluding to the somewhat ragged appearance of the blossoms. There are several species of *Senecio* in the Poudre drainage, but none so tall and showy as these.

Delphiniums are well known from the horticultural varieties we grow in gardens. With our usual fascination with names, we discovered that the name is based on the Latin word for a dolphin, *delphinis*, a curious association presumably suggested by an imagined resemblance of the nectaries to a dolphin. Its alternative name, larkspur, is believed to be descriptive of the blossoms, the splayed petals suggesting the forward toes of a lark, the spur the long back toe. None of this is very helpful to ranchers, who heartily dislike larkspurs of any kind, since cattle like to eat the young foliage and often become ill, sometimes dying if they eat too much. Oddly, sheep are immune to the poisons and have sometimes been used to clear larkspur from a pasture before admitting the cattle. Livestock grazing on national forest land are always at risk of overconsuming toxins in the diverse vegetation they encounter in their wanderings.

Following the Killpecker trail below the springs, one passes through shadowed forests of lodgepole pine with a uniform ground cover of broom huckleberry (also called whortleberry, bilberry, or grouseberry). It is unusual to find berries on these bushes; evidently they often do not set fruit, and when they do the berries are quickly consumed by rodents. The berries are tiny and it would take a great many to make a pie. Indians used to dry the berries and use them in soups or in pemmican. Early settlers used the leaves to make tea, as they did the leaves of a variety of plants.

Through the forest one sees many piles of pinecone fragments, a result of the work of pine squirrels, and it is unusual to walk very far without being challenged by one of these feisty animals. The pine squirrel of the Rockies is actually a subspecies of the red squirrel of the eastern states, although it is predominantly grayish. *Tamiasciurus hudsonicus fremonti* is an imposing scientific name for so small a squirrel, but it is appropriate: *Tamia-sciurus* is Greek for "hoarder-squirrel" (hoarder of evergreen cones, in this case); *hudsonicus* refers to Hudson's Bay, well within the range of this cold-adapted animal; and *fremonti* is of course for John Charles Frémont, for whom so many western animals and plants are named. These were favorites of Enos Mills, who called them Frémont squirrels and succeeded in taming several, even though normally they have little use for anyone who invades their territories. As Mills says, if you approach "he may come down on a low limb nearby and give you as torrential and as abusive a 'cussing' as trespasser ever received from irate owner."

Pine squirrels do not hibernate, though they may sleep in their nests through winter storms. Much of the summer and autumn is spent harvesting and caching food supplies, mostly pine or fir cones but sometimes fungi and berries. They have the curious habit of picking mushrooms and drying them on limbs of trees; when they are dry, they are added to the winter stocks of food. Like many rodents, they also gnaw on bones and antlers, apparently obtaining calcium and phosphorus from this source. Most of their feeding is done at one site, resulting in a pile of cone fragments and other scraps, a "kitchen midden." Cones, mushrooms, bones, and berries are sometimes stored in the middens, sometimes in other hiding places in the ground or in logs.

Having stored a winter's supply, pine squirrels defend their territories vigorously. Usually these are one to two acres in size, enough to assure a good crop of cones. The squirrels are remarkably agile as they leap from tree to tree; leaps of twenty feet are not uncommon, though they prefer to live in dense trees where such leaps are unnecessary. After clipping off several cones, they descend to the ground and collect them, always appearing in a great hurry. In the spring territorial borders are relaxed, and males enter territories owned by females. From two to six young are born in June in a nest of grasses and leaves in a hollow tree or amidst dense branches. Although pine squirrels are favorite food of martens and goshawks, their numbers are controlled more by the abundance of cones than by predators. Lodgepole pine forests in the Poudre basin present a relatively dependable source of cones and almost any hike in the high country is likely to be enlivened by these hardy and energetic animals.

The birds that chipper in the trees along the Killpecker Trail are more often than not mountain chickadees. These are easily distinguished from the black-capped chickadees of the plains by the pale line over the eye. They are among the tamest of birds, and in the winter will often take sunflower seeds from one's hand. In the summer they are ardent insectivores, and when spruce budworms are abundant they take them in great numbers. They will nest in almost any cavity they can find, and if disturbed will sit very tightly on the nest, often hissing and fluttering their wings. The female lays an unusually large clutch of eggs, usually seven to twelve.

Mountain chickadees bear the scientific name *Parus gambeli*, named for a Philadelphia naturalist, William Gambel, who, at twenty-three, joined a party of trappers so that he could explore the West for birds and plants. Eventually he reached California, on the way discovering not only the chickadees but also Gambel's quail, Gambel's oak, and several other plants and birds. On a second trip to California in 1849, when he was 28, Gambel tried to cross the Sierras in midwinter, but he stumbled into Rose's Bar, on the Feather River, suffering from exhaustion. He died of typhoid fever a few days later. One of his fellow travelers described him as an amiable, excellent fellow. It is good that he left a bit of himself in the name of one of our commonest birds, also in its own way amiable and excellent.

The Killpecker Trail is not only a good place to become familiar with small birds such as chickadees but also with one of the mountains' largest birds. Ravens are birds of tall forests and rocky cliffs. They are experts at finding food in the coldest and most barren places, either carrion, small mammals, the eggs and young of other birds, or occasionally berries or other plant food. They are the largest of the passerine or "song" birds, with a wingspan comparable to that of many hawks. Often they ride on updrafts, like hawks, and at times seem to ride motionless in the air. Courting pairs sometimes soar with their wingtips touching and perform various acrobatics. In the words of Arthur Cleveland Bent:

"With the springtime urge of love-making, the otherwise sedate and dignified ravens let themselves go and indulge in most interesting and thrilling flight maneuvers and vocal performances. Chasing each other about in rapid flight, they dive, tumble, twist, turn somersaults, roll over sidewise, or mount high in the air and soar in great circles on their broad, black wings. Their powers of flight shown in these playful antics are no less surprising than the variety of their melodious love notes, soft modulations of their well-known croaks, varied with many clucking and gurgling sounds. Their exuberant spirits seem to be overflowing at this season."

Ravens mate for life and may live for thirty years. Pairs have a home territory which they patrol for food, sharing carcasses or whatever other food they can find. Although ravens sometimes harass large animals and will kill rabbits and other small mammals, they are remarkably cautious when approaching a newly found carcass. They land some distance away, approach slowly and when close to it jump up and down while flapping their wings. After a while they may peck at the carcass, then resume their jumping behavior. In a provocative essay, "Why Do Ravens Fear Their Food?", Bernd Heinrich, of the University of Vermont, has speculated that this behavior may have evolved to insure that ravens do not approach a sleeping or sick animal that might attack them. In his words, "The jumping-jack maneuvers may function in eliciting a reaction from live animals, letting the approaching bird know whether or not it is safe to try to feed." Dr. Heinrich found that hand-reared, inexperienced ravens behaved in the same way, so evidently this is not a learned response.

Ravens do not attain sexual maturity for several years, and juveniles and unmated individuals are nonterritorial and often roost together at night. Territorial pairs feed quietly on a carcass, but when the food is discovered by one of these vagrants he may recruit others by "yelling," a type of call very different from the usual hoarse "croak" of these birds. Only by recruiting a crowd can the vagrants overcome the defenses of the resident pair and share in the feast. Even so, the residents take the best pieces of carrion, asserting their dominance by standing tall and fluffing out their feathers, while the vagrants draw their heads into their necks submissively and make the best of it. Only by force of numbers can the vagrants be assured of a meal—an unusual example of competitors calling upon rivals to help them gain access to a resource.

These, too, are recent discoveries of Bernd Heinrich, who observed the birds from a blind or a nearby treetop, using a great many carcasses and chunks of slaughterhouse offal to attract the birds. In order to follow individual birds, he captured forty-three of them and marked them with tags, and two were fitted with radio transmitters. After many days in the cold winter woods, he developed a genuine affection for these often maligned birds. Because of their black plumage and hankering for corpses, ravens have acquired a reputation as birds of death, as in Poe's haunting poem. To those of us who look forward to seeing ravens riding the air currents or to hearing them call across a valley, these are very much birds of life, a life that seems to revel in the wild forests and crystalline air of the mountains.

Too soon the Killpecker Trail ends at its junction with the Deadman Hill road, where the stream joins the North Fork. But there will be other days and other trails.

The Cache la Poudre Today

By a mountain stream, "it is impossible to believe that one will ever be tired or old. Every sense applauds it." So wrote Wallace Stegner in *The Sound of Mountain Water*. Yet the mountain-born streams of the West are precisely what have made human endeavors possible in this semiarid land. Hence a common alternate view, that any water flowing downstream is "water wasted." This is a constant dilemma of the West, one that pits environmentalists against developers; those who opt for clean air and water against those that press for more industry and jobs; those who treasure the serenity of forests and streamsides against those who delight in roaring cross-country in off-road vehicles; those who respect the integrity of the plants, animals, and soil of natural communities against those who see these as resources to be developed. The waters of the Cache la Poudre were diverted soon after the first white settlers arrived, and they remain vital to agriculture, industry, and family life in the area. Yet the basin remains well forested, reasonably rich in wildlife, and drained by a stream that still retains, at least in the canyon, enough of its original character to justify its designation as Wild and Scenic. To a degree, those of us who live in the Poudre basin have the best of both worlds. Retaining a balance may not be easy as the human population along the Front Range continues to grow. ...

For people who live by or who visit the Cache la Poudre, these are the best of times in the best of places. No longer must they endure the hardships of the pioneers; the wildlife is no longer a threat, but something to cherish. There is water for everyone. Roads and trails make most parts of the basin easily accessible, yet great sections are preserved in seminatural condition by being part of Rocky Mountain National Park or Roosevelt National Forest, the latter including four wilderness areas. A major part of the Poudre and its South Fork have been designated Wild and Scenic, and The Nature Conservancy has preserved Phantom Canyon on the North Fork.

No matter that the Poudre is very different than it was before whites arrived. Seven transmountain diversions add "foreign" water during the warmer months; there are eleven mountain reservoirs, innumerable plains reservoirs, and a network of irrigation ditches that defy comprehension. Some of these ditches and reservoirs actually increase diversity of species by providing wetlands not previously available. And wilderness, as we all know, is a relative term. As Wallace Stegner has said, "the conservationists who created our national wilderness system knew from the beginning that by this date [1964], wilderness in America is an approximation only."

Early settlers and tie cutters found the streams to be filled with native greenback cutthroat trout and the forests sometimes too abundantly filled with game. "The lumbermen of the Upper Poudre lead a wild and adventurous life," reported *The Denver News* on July 28, 1875. "When the winter snows drive game down from the range, their cabins are actually surrounded by night and by day. Then every cabin is an arsenal, and guns are loaded for protection as well as for game. Mountain lions roar around them."

When ranchers began to run cattle in the upper Poudre valleys, they became sufficiently alarmed to press the state legislature for protection from predators. In 1889 a law was passed providing a bounty of one dollar for each wolf or coyote killed and a bounty of ten dollars for each bear or mountain lion. The law attracted professional hunters, and within a few years the threat of predators was gone. Populations of deer, elk, bighorn sheep, turkeys, and other game birds and mammals were also greatly decimated over the next few decades.

Some of the larger mammals of the Poudre are now extinct (though still surviving elsewhere). Bison now occur only in fenced pastures, and gray wolves, grizzly bears, and wolverines are gone. Many would agree that this is for the best. These animals are potentially dangerous to humans, and most of us would prefer not to confront a grizzly on a trail near our homes. Too bad we cannot get rid of a few other, lesser nuisances, such as wood ticks, mountain pine beetles, and mistletoe. However, the elimination of any species has ecological consequences, however subtle, so it is dangerous to draft a list of species we could do without. ...

There is much to be learned about what species occur in the Poudre basin and what roles they play in the complex webs of life. Researchers at universities along the Front Range, as well as those at the Colorado Division of Wildlife and the U.S. Forest Service, have been studying the fauna and flora of the area for many years. They will not soon run out of things to study. Entomologists by inclination and training, we have been studying wasps that prey on diverse insects and spiders. One of these proved to be an exclusive predator on western tent caterpillars that disfigure and sometimes kill bushes and trees in the foothills each spring—bushes that deer require for browse. Another preys on defoliating larvae such as those of the spruce budworms that periodically cause the death of many Douglas-firs. These and others play little-appreciated roles in regulating populations of destructive insects that might, in their absence, do far more damage than they commonly do. Research of this nature is usually done as a labor of love, for there is little public support for solving problems not of obvious and immediate importance. Meaningful research must usually be conducted in places that are relatively undisturbed. Many of the wasps we study nest in the ground and cannot survive in places trampled by cattle, for example.

Why is it important to learn more about the fauna and flora of the Poudre basin—or anywhere else? Most basically it is because we humans have taken our place in a world containing tens of thousands of other creatures that evolved along with us and impinge on our lives in innumerable and often unexpected ways. Yet the natural world is inexorably slipping away as our numbers and our desires for luxuries-become-necessities expand. That we should let it disappear to the point that we live (or try to live) in a wholly artificial environment—without ever having fully inventoried and understood the world we have replaced—is to thinking people, well, unthinkable.

Of course one does not need to be an entomologist, an ornithologist, or even a biologist in the broadest sense to appreciate and enjoy the Cache la Poudre and the wonderful country it drains. To sensate persons, there are not only the pleasures of the seasons—the first spring beauties appearing where the snows have melted back; the return of the nighthawks in June; the turning of the aspens; the first fresh snow on the peaks—but there are always surprises—a wildflower never seen before, occasioning a rush to the field guides; a snowy egret on a plains reservoir; a glimpse of a marten in a subalpine forest. To persons who crave a less passive experience in the wild, there are trails for vigorous hiking and cross-country skiing, the river to be rafted or kayaked, and of course hunting and fishing. Nature is inexhaustibly rewarding. That this is so sometimes escapes the attention of those who live in the mushrooming cities that nestle beneath their canopies of carbon monoxide and particulates. All too often, nature is seen merely as a source of fuels, minerals, building materials, and space for shopping malls.

Nature does have other values, not only recreational but also aesthetic, scientific, symbolic, even religious, and should also be valued for its future resource potential—the genetic diversity we may someday need to enrich our food supplies; still to be discovered natural chemicals that may serve as medicines or natural pesticides; examples of living in harsh environments that may someday serve as models for us. That nature has intrinsic values— that species and ecosystems may have their own "right to life"— is a thought alien to most people, though being eloquently espoused by a few. Is it too much to hope that the majority may someday be convinced of the need for an ethic of the environment, a belief that we are part of a complex web of life that can be violated only so far before we find that we have irretrievably violated our own humanity?

Spring has come again to the Cache la Poudre. Mountain blue-birds flash on the hillsides and chipmunks scurry among the rocks. The aspens are hung with catkins, and on warm slopes pasque flowers and Easter daisies are in bloom. Once again free of ice, the river whispers quietly, as if saving its energies for the tumult soon to come, when the snows melt in the high country. Then the stream will speak more loudly, reminding us that it is the architect of this canyon, the wherewithal of everything that lives here. There will be rafters riding its currents, anglers prob-ing its pools, hikers exploring its side canyons, a cohabitation of man and nature that is all too rare in a society that often seems to spin upon itself, forgetful of its heritage and its ultimate suste-nance. Summer's exuberance will pass; autumn will bring gold to the aspen leaves, winter its arctic blasts; then another spring. Whatever new directions human history may by then have taken, the river will be there, the pines soughing in the wind, the birds singing the same songs, the wildflowers attracting bees and setting seed. And we shall need them.

14

The Birds of Australia

Persons attracted to the natural world are invariably drawn to Australia, its flora and fauna so distinctive that one might think "two Creators must have been at work" (Charles Darwin's words). I have been to Australia four times, for an equivalent of about two years, and have added a bit to knowledge of its insect fauna. In 1979 Mary Alice received a grant from the American Association of University Women to write a book about Australian natural history for Americans, and together we wrote such a book, published by the Smithsonian Institution in 1983. Here is one chapter, slightly abridged.

A NORTH AMERICAN is likely to gain the impression that Australian birds are, on the whole, rather larger, noisier, and more flamboyant than he is used to, and also, at times, a good deal tamer. At our home in Indooroopilly, not far from the Brisbane River, we were constantly surprised by the variety and abundance of bird life—all the way from the tiny redbacked fairy wrens foraging in the hedges to brush turkeys scratching in the dead leaves we were too lazy to rake up. Except during periods of extreme drought in the Interior, there is not a habitat that does not have its own complex of birds. And learning the birds in suburban Brisbane didn't help us much when we visited a rain forest, or a water hole in the Center!

Needless to say, a well-informed bird lover or a professional ornithologist (and we are neither) finds Australia a continent of vast rewards. It is true that Australia has fewer species of birds than any other continent—a consequence of the fact that it is the smallest continent and the one with the least varied climate and topography. The mountainous island of New Guinea, though only a tenth the size of Australia, has about as many species of birds. There are about six hundred that breed in Australia, plus several introduced species and over a hundred casuals. The novelty of the fauna arises from the fact that well over half the resident species occur nowhere else, and a number of major groups (families) are restricted to the Australian region.

Equally striking to Americans is the fact that several groups are completely absent. There are no woodpeckers, for example, no jays, no shrikes, no pheasants, no hummingbirds. On the other hand, some familiar groups have "gone wild" and have evolved curious birds not at all familiar. Australian cuckoos are a strange lot, and flycatchers are so diverse that some are called "fantails" and others "robins" (no relation to the American or European robin). And the laughing kookaburra is in fact a kingfisher that has abandoned the water and turned to a diet of snakes, lizards, and insects.

The earliest Europeans in Australia often thought of birds primarily as a source of food. Sealers learned to eat shearwaters ("mutton birds") on the southeast coast and offshore islands; settlers shot ducks and doves; and cockatoo stew often sustained explorers in the Outback. Credit for the first scientific study of birds belongs to John Gould, an Englishman who had completed a five-volume *Birds of Europe* before visiting Australia for eighteen months in 1838–40.

Gould's Australian experiences were marked by tragedy. While he was birding on the islands of Bass Strait, one of his boatmen accidentally shot himself; Johnston Drummond, son of the government botanist of Western Australia, was murdered by aborigines while collecting birds for him; and John Gilbert, his major collector, was speared by aborigines in northern Queensland while accompanying Ludwig Leichhardt on his expedition from Brisbane to the coast of Northern Territory. Worse still, Gould's talented wife Elizabeth died shortly after her return to England, at the age of thirty-seven, after bearing him six children and completing over six hundred paintings for his books. Gould employed a number of other artists, among whom was Edward Lear, of *Book of Nonsense* fame. (Lear was, in fact, a distinguished bird portraitist; his illustrations of parrots have recently been republished—selling for $1,100 a volume.)

To support his research and publications, Gould sold his volumes by subscription and also sold mounted birds and mammals. His 1,800 Australian bird specimens were offered to the British Museum for one thousand pounds, but were refused. They were later purchased by an American, Edward Wilson, and donated to The Academy of Natural Sciences of Philadelphia. Gould's *Birds of Australia* appeared in eight volumes, from 1840 to 1848, and contained 681 carefully prepared plates.

To the visitor, it is the uniquely Australian groups that prove most intriguing. One of the most abundant of these groups is a family called the Cracticidae [a word appropriately based on the Greek word *kraktikos,* noisy], which includes a number of rather large, black-and-white birds often seen in parks and suburban areas. Chief among these are the Australian magpies, which have nothing in common with the American or European magpies except that they are black and white. The song of the magpie is one of the most characteristic sounds of early morning, impossible to describe but rather like a somewhat amorphous tune played on a slightly wheezy alto recorder. Magpies are robust birds with large beaks, which they use for probing the soil for insects. They are fairly long-lived, and pairs stay together for several years, but only after they are six to eight years old do they usually nest successfully in a strongly defended territory. Even though magpies are normally rather tame birds, during the nesting season they defend their territories vigorously against other magpies and even against other birds, dogs, cats, and sometimes human intruders.

An aroused magpie produces loud warning calls, and if further provoked will swoop at the intruder and sometimes lash at it with its powerful beak. There are numerous records of humans receiving scalp wounds from them. In one spring month in Perth, thirty-two magpies were shot following attacks on people. Actually, shooting them is at best only temporarily satisfying, as prime territories are quickly filled by other magpies. A better solution is to heed the warning calls and stay away from aggressive pairs during the spring breeding season. Magpies are, on the balance, friendly and desirable birds, consuming quantities of noxious insects and brightening the dawn with their caroling.

Close relatives of the magpies, the butcher birds also have a somewhat unfortunate reputation (and an unsuitable name). They are reputed to impale their insect prey on a twig while they tear it apart with their hooked beaks. Butcher birds resemble rather slender magpies and have an even more remarkable song that often carries a great distance. In fact, the several species of butcher birds are perhaps the premier songsters of Australia (the much less commonly encountered lyrebirds excepted). On our first trip into the bush we camped by a remote salt pan in central Western Australia. Each morning we were awakened by a complex melody, infinitely melancholy, we thought, and thoroughly suitable for that desolate landscape. We learned later that it was a butcher bird and that individuals often develop quite different songs. According to one bird book, the pied butcher bird often suggests the opening bars of Beethoven's Fifth Symphony, but to us butcher birds suggested a flautist trying to find just the right combination of notes to do justice to the morning.

To this same group belong the currawongs, which are rather like large, elongate magpies that prefer forested areas. Their calls are loud and clear but less varied than those of their relatives the magpies and butcher birds. In several of the national parks in which we camped, flocks of currawongs descended upon us, staring at us with their great yellow eyes and loudly demanding to be fed. We soon found out that it was best to ignore them so that they would fly to someone else's camp and relieve our harried ear drums.

Another black-and-white bird, which looks rather like a slender magpie although it is not related, is the mudlark or magpie-lark. These are prim and elegant birds, not the least bit larklike and displaying only a rather shrill "pee-wit" call. At times, male and female perch side by side and call rapidly and alternately, each raising its wings over its head as it calls. Mudlarks are fiercely protective of their nests, and are often seen pursuing crows or hawks many times their size. We found mudlarks common almost everywhere we went in Australia except in desert country. Since mud is used in constructing their nests, they do not stray far from a source of water. The mudlark family, like the cracticids, is restricted to Australia and New Guinea.

There seems to be no end of black-and-white birds in Australia. Besides mudlarks, currawongs, butcher birds, and magpies, there are white-winged choughs, pied honeyeaters, pied cormorants, pied geese, and a number of black-and-white species of flycatchers. Even the famous black swans have white patches on their wings, and white pelicans have black! Why Australian birds seem to specialize in black and white is anybody's guess.

We have mentioned the lyrebirds, which belong to a group having no close relatives in any part of the world. There are two species, both confined to forests of southeastern Australia. Lyrebirds are chicken-sized, brownish, ground-dwelling birds. The males have long, silver tail plumes framed with distinctive brown and white lyre-shaped feathers.

Lyrebirds were evidently once quite common, for in her classic *Childhood at Brindabella*, Miles Franklin speaks of gullies (not far from the present city of Canberra) as being "alive with these fey creatures." But she also tells of trappers coming out of the mountains with long poles strung with lyrebirds on the way to market, many to provide feathers for ladies' hats in other parts of the world. These remarkable birds can still be seen in a few reserves if one is sufficiently patient and is afoot at the right time and place. Most Australians are familiar with lyrebirds chiefly through their appearance on their ten-cent coins!

During courtship, the male lyrebird struts and sings from a mound of soil he has prepared, spreading his remarkable tail feathers so that they extend over the top of his head. The song is loud and brilliantly melodic, and woven into it are the calls of many other birds that occur in the area. Since males are competing for the resident females, it is perhaps to their advantage to achieve as much variety as possible in their songs, and they do this by "borrowing" from other species ("liarbirds," one wag has called them). Lyrebirds breed in the wintertime, so these imitations cause no particular confusion among these other species, which have not yet begun to court. Male lyrebirds are polygynous—mating with whatever females they are able to attract to the several display mounds in their territory.

We had spent nearly two full years in Australia before we were able to fulfill a dream to see and hear lyrebirds in their native habitat. On a cool winter morning we visited Tidbinbilla Nature Reserve, near Canberra, arriving well before the influx of noisy people on holiday. And there they were.

A mating system remotely like that of lyrebirds is practiced by members of still another group restricted to Australia (and in this case also New Guinea), the bower birds. These birds have no elegant tail feathers, but as artisans they are unsurpassed. There are some eighteen species, but by far the best known of these is the satin bower bird, so called because of the uniform satin-blue plumage of the males. Like lyrebirds, the male selects a display arena in the bush, but it is of very different form, as the male builds an "avenue" five or six inches wide and about a foot long, flanked by walls ten to fourteen inches high composed of carefully selected sticks. The floor is covered with twigs and grass, and the threshold is decorated with flowers, berries, feathers, and (since the advent of Western man) with bits of glass, paper, bottle caps, and the like. Blue objects seem to be preferred to those of any other color, and neighboring birds will often pilfer especially desirable blue objects from one another's bowers. The males paint their bowers with a mixture of saliva and plant juices, using a stick as a paintbrush. Thus they are rightly considered among the very few animals that use tools.

During the breeding season, the males display in their bowers, and females are attracted to them. Males posture, flutter their wings, and produce a variety of sounds, including fragments of songs borrowed from other birds. From time to time they pick up objects from their caches and hold them in their beaks. Following mating, the female establishes a nest elsewhere and rears the young with no help from the male.

The satin bower bird is an inhabitant of moist eastern forests, but that is by no means true of all members of this group. The spotted bower bird of the dry interior is said to be an even more remarkable mimic, often including in his repertory human-made sounds such as the sharpening of a scythe or the twanging of a fence wire (also, it is said, the barking of a dog or the crackling of a bush fire). The bower of this species is not unlike that of the satin bower bird, but it is decorated with green and white objects, including unripe berries, bits of bone, and petals of white flowers.

Francis Ratcliffe tells of a tame spotted bower bird that was presented with a multicolored children's marble, which it promptly rejected. Twice more the marble was placed in the bower, and twice more removed. On the fourth occasion, the bird picked up the marble in its beak and dropped it in a nearby river. The spotted bower bird has been known to steal jewelry from windowsills and has even been reported to have taken a glass eye from a bedside! Jock Marshall and Russell Drysdale, in their book *Journey Among Men*, tell of a spotted bower bird that stole the ignition keys from a parked car. "The aggrieved owner was shrewd enough to go to the nearest bower, where he found them."

In the Northern Territory, we were lucky enough to come upon the bower of the great bower bird, its floor decorated solely with large white snail shells. But it was the dry season, and the birds were not to be seen. However, in a rain forest in northern Queensland our fortunes improved and we spotted several pairs of rifle birds, their iridescent blue-green throats and tail feathers sparkling like jewels in shafts of sunlight that penetrated the canopy. Rifle birds are not bower birds, but belong to a related group, the birds of paradise. These birds reach their fullest expression in New Guinea and adjacent islands, where the elegant plumes and curious courtship displays of the males stretch one's credulity.

In lyrebirds, bower birds, and birds of paradise the males expend much effort in seducing the female, but little or none in caring for the offspring. By contrast, in birds such as the emus and mound-builders, much of the care of the young falls to the males. The emu is the Australian equivalent of the ostrich, and is second only to the ostrich in size, often standing six feet in height and weighing as much as 120 pounds. Like the ostrich the female emu lays huge eggs, measuring some five inches and weighing well over a pound—yet she lays eight or ten such eggs. Presumably she is so exhausted she must take time to recuperate, leaving the male to incubate the eggs and care for the chicks.

Emus are unpopular with graziers, and they are heartily detested by wheat growers, since they are grain feeders and are able to cover a good deal of ground in their search for food. Nevertheless they are still fairly abundant in parts of the Outback, and it is not uncommon to see an adult male followed by a brood of striped chicks.

The emus belong to a group of ancient, flightless birds called the ratites, a group that also includes the cassowary, a shy inhabitant of the forests of New Guinea and extreme northeastern Australia, as well as the ostrich of Africa, the rhea of South America, and the famous kiwi of New Zealand. The extinct moas of New Zealand and the elephant birds of Madagascar were also ratites.

Fortunately the emus are nowadays not widely esteemed as food. Not so with the aborigines and early settlers. Captain John Hunter, the second governor of New South Wales, dined on emu and thought it "delicious meat. ... A party of five, myself included, dined on a side-bone of it most scrumptiously." When explorer Ludwig Leichhardt was deep in the bush, he roasted emus over an open fire and collected the oil dripping from them to use in lubricating his firearms. He also rubbed oil on his body as an antirheumatic and for what he called its "slightly exciting properties." [There are now numerous emu farms in the United States, and both emu oil and flesh are being marketed.]

The lot of male mound-builders is even more strenuous than that of the emus. These birds lay their eggs in huge piles of earth and detritus measuring from twelve to fifteen feet in diameter and as much as three feet high. The mallee fowl, the best known of the three species of mound-builders, lives in scrubby, semidesert areas of the Interior. Male and female cooperate building a pit during the winter months; into this pit they scrape leaf litter; then, after waiting for a rain, they cover the litter with the soil they have excavated. As the season advances, the moist litter begins to ferment and produce heat. The female then begins to lay eggs, the male standing by and opening the mound each time she is ready to lay. In all she may lay thirty or more eggs, at intervals of from five to ten days.

Each egg requires seven to twelve weeks' incubation at the proper temperature—ninety degrees Fahrenheit—and it is the male's job to see that this temperature is maintained. He does this by altering the thickness of the layer of soil over the fermenting material around the eggs. Early in the cycle, fermentation is strong, and the male must open the mound early in the morning to permit cooling, then refill it before the sun's heat becomes too great. During the summer, fermentation declines but the sun's heat is intense, necessitating a thick layer of soil for insulation during the day. In the fall, reduced heat both from fermentation and from the sun requires that the mound be opened for variable periods during the day.

How does the male measure the temperature of the mound so accurately? Harry Frith, of the Australian Division of Wildlife Research, found that the male inserts his bill into the mound periodically and withdraws it full of soil. He then performs whatever needs to be done, suggesting that he has "tasted" the temperature with his tongue. When Dr. Frith artificially heated the mounds by installing electric heating elements, the birds quickly detected the changes and began cooling activities.

Because of the intervals between egg laying, plus the long incubation period, the male is kept busy virtually half the year, and must have difficulty getting far enough away from the mound to find adequate food for himself. A hard life! When the eggs hatch one by one, the hatchlings merely push their way out and wander off into the bush, usually without ever seeing their parents.

The mallee fowl is now a relatively rare bird, but once it was widely distributed in drier parts of the continent, where its eggs provided a welcome addition to the diet of the aborigines and early settlers. We had an opportunity to visit the nest of a mallee fowl in Wyperfeld National Park, in northwestern Victoria. Unfortunately, the male scurried off into the bush before we could see much of him, but it was nevertheless a treat to see such an unusual structure.

Another mound-builder, the brush turkey, became much more familiar to us and on one occasion stole food from our campsite when we were only a few yards away. Brush turkeys are impressive creatures, about the size of the quite unrelated domestic turkeys, with a naked red head and neck and glossy black plumage elsewhere. The males have a bright yellow, loose collar of skin between neck and breast, and this flaps about conspicuously as they chase each other through the bush. Altogether a striking bird, the brush turkey has a domestic life not unlike that of the mallee fowl, although brush turkeys are inhabitants of eastern forests rather than the dry interior.

It is hard to know where to stop when talking about Australian birds. A traveler from North America is certain to be impressed by the parrots, noisy and garishly colored as they are. All the way from sparrow-sized budgerigars to giant black cockatoos, they form a major element on the Australian scene. Species occurring in the Interior often flock to waterholes or cattle troughs, and in coastal areas parrots are readily attracted to feeding stations, where they form a surrealistic tumult of color.

As we look back on our years in Australia, they seem to be punctuated by parrots—rainbow lorikeets chattering in the trees of our back yard; crimson rosellas landing on our shoulders and cameras when we tried to photograph them; a great flock of sulphur-crested cockatoos that screeched so interminably that we finally fled a woodland in Northern Territory, almost screaming ourselves. Perhaps the biggest surprise came in the mountains of Tasmania, when we were hiking in a midsummer snow squall and watched green rosellas gamboling in the antarctic beeches. It seemed incongruous, to say the least, to see parrots in a snow storm.

Parrots occur throughout the tropical and subtropical parts of the world, though nowhere so diverse as in Australia. Thus we have departed a bit from our plan to discuss groups that are more or less restricted to Australia. Of these, by far the largest is the family of honeyeaters (Meliphagidae—which is Latin for exactly that). Honeyeaters also occur in New Guinea and parts of the East Indies, but nowhere else. It is probably no coincidence that this large group, with over seventy Australian species, has evolved on a continent dominated by trees having an abundance of nectar-bearing flowers, especially eucalyptus. In fact, trees and birds probably evolved together, the eucalyptus depending upon honeyeaters as major instruments of pollination.

As the name implies, these birds are specialists at extracting nectar from blossoms, to a certain extent filling the niche occupied by hummingbirds in America. They are, however, not a bit like hummingbirds; the smaller ones are suggestive of warblers or vireos, the larger ones perhaps reminiscent of cuckoos. To a non-specialist, honeyeaters seem a diverse group, all the way from tiny ones no more than four inches long to others measuring twenty inches; all the way from the flashy scarlet honeyeater to the drab and even rather ugly friarbirds.

The honeyeater family is usually defined on the basis of the slender and somewhat down-curved beak and brushlike tongue. Some specialists believe the group is not really a natural one, but rather a diverse lot of unrelated birds that have all evolved similar mechanisms for feeding on nectar. Whatever the case, honey-eaters are very much a part of the Australian scene, and we had a good deal of fun trying to identify them.

One we did learn to recognize quickly was the noisy miner—though we never did learn why it is called a miner, since it does not seem to mine in anything. Noisy miners are rather tame, robin-sized honeyeaters that abound in parks and suburbs in eastern Australia. Only recently has their remarkable social life been brought to light, largely through the efforts of Douglas Dow, of the University of Queensland.

Miners live in large colonies, often of several hundred individuals. The colony territory is vigorously defended against other bird species and even against goannas, wallabies, dogs, and sometimes even people. A number of kinds of birds are recorded as having been killed by mobs of miners. Most of the species mobbed are not predators—in the way that various birds will mob crows, which feed on their eggs—but rather aggression seems to clear the area of birds and other creatures that might compete for food with the miner colony.

Miner colonies, Dr. Dow found, are further divided into "coteries," each consisting of several males which collectively occupy and to some extent defend a certain part of the area in which several females build their nests. Members of a coterie often feed and sleep together, and at times indulge in a "corroboree," greeting each other boisterously while moving their wings slowly up and down. Within each group there is a dominance hierarchy or "peck order." Dominant males assert themselves by calling and by assuming a horizontal body stance and "outstaring" their rivals, their apparent eye size being increased by a bare yellow patch of skin. When we lived in Brisbane suburbs, our house opened onto a group of trees occupied by a troop of noisy miners, who sometimes had so much to fuss about that we had to shout to converse.

Males of a coterie visit the nests in the area, built by the females, and the females mate with them more or less indiscriminately. By such "prostitution," each female gathers about her several males, which assist in removing fecal pellets from the nest and in feeding the young. As the fledglings grow, the number of visits by the males increases, up to as many as fifty visits an hour, involving up to twenty-two different males (though usually fewer). The males may provide as much as 80 percent of the food required by the rapidly growing young. Evidently there are many more males than females, and by becoming a "helper" a male is likely, in the long run, to be helping to rear his own offspring. Miners are long-lived, and many of the helpers are young males which, with experience, may become dominant in the coterie and likely to father a higher percentage of the offspring.

Noisy miners are by no means the only Australian birds living in social groups in which some individuals are helpers. Recent studies have shown that the widely distributed rainbow bee-eaters and the blue wrens also have social groups. Bee-eaters are relatives of the kingfishers, but look more like orange and green swallows in their graceful acrobatic flights after insects (although they are quite distinctive with the central pair of tail feathers projecting). They nest, however, not in trees but in the ground, and especially banks. There they dig tunnels up to three feet long, and at the end lay five to seven eggs. Once hatched, the young are fed by several adults.

More detailed studies have been done on the blue wrens, which are common inhabitants of parks and gardens in southeastern Australia. It has been observed that breeding pairs are usually assisted in caring for the young by several others, usually but not always their own offspring from earlier broods. Members of a group sleep and feed together and may even preen one another. Blue wrens are not nearly as long-lived as miners, and do not survive generally beyond five or six years. By serving as helpers for a year or two, both males and females gain in experience and are in a position to take over a familiar, prime territory when their parents pass on.

Incidentally, Australian wrens are not true wrens at all, but belong to another uniquely Australian family, the Maluridae (often called "fairy wrens" to distinguish them from true wrens). These are tiny birds with upturned tails, and one cannot blame the early settlers for dubbing them "wrens" even though they differ in many ways from the wrens of the Northern Hemisphere. These are among the most elegant of birds, notable for their iridescent colors, which in dim light often seem black but in sunlight shine brilliantly. The names of the various species suggest their plumage: blue wren, turquoise wren, purple-backed wren, lilac-crowned wren, red-backed wren. In one of our study sites south of Brisbane, we became specially acquainted with the variegated wren, a delightful splashing of blue, red, black, and white that often came popping out of the bushes only a few feet from us.

From the sublime to the ridiculous—the "laughing" kookaburra, the most famous of Australian birds. But in fact it is not that much of a transition. Not only is the kookaburra a much more admirable bird than its vocalizations suggest, but it, too, lives in groups containing helpers. Curiously, it was an American, Veronica Parry, who first studied the kookaburra's social system critically. She found that many pairs were assisted by from one to five individuals, of either sex.

Each pair occupies territory that is defended by "laughing" duets, trios, quartets, or whatever. One display at territorial borders is called a "trapeze display," since the birds take turns flying back and forth between two fixed points, timed so that two of them pass in midair. In the meantime, a group on a neighboring territory may be chorusing and trapezing similarly. In general, larger groups are able to maintain a larger territory because of the greater intensity of their displays. Helpers provide up to 60 percent of the food for the nestlings. Again, it may be more advantageous for a yearling to help defend a territory he or she may inherit one day than to "go it alone."

The "song" of the kookaburra must be heard to be believed. It is usually performed with one or more other individuals, one beginning with a chuckle followed by a series of "hoo-hoos." Soon others join in with hoo-hoos and ha-has in marvelous disharmony until the forest quakes with "laughter." Dawn in forested parts of Australia—even in city suburbs—is not complete without a chorus of kookaburras. According to one aboriginal legend, the dawn chorus is a signal for the sky people to light the great fire that will warm the earth by day.

Many a time we have been wakened in the bush by the too-early calls of the kookaburra; but it is hard to bear a grudge against so marvelous a bird. In some of the national parks, kookaburras have become quite tame. On more than one occasion we have had these handsome birds perch on the edge of our picnic table and follow us with their eyes while we ate, and even help themselves to a bit of sausage when our attention was diverted elsewhere.

Although this berserk kingfisher lives on insects, lizards, and snakes and is rightly considered beneficial, it does usurp tree holes from other species and also sometimes feeds on nestlings of other birds. Northern Australia is the home of the beautiful blue-winged kookaburra, a slightly less frenetic species that also lives in small groups containing helpers.

The question is sometimes asked why Australia has so many birds that have helpers at the nest, individuals that sacrifice reproduction (at least for a time) to assist in rearing brothers and sisters or sometimes nonrelatives. We have mentioned only a few; there are also babblers, thornbills, magpies, and still others. Undoubtedly, group feeding often enhances survival of the offspring, and group defense assures a larger and better feeding territory. This may be especially important in the variable climate of Australia, where it may be critical to take advantage of benign conditions, when the next year may bring a drought or a cyclone. Prolonged drought or extreme heat waves may cause birds to cease breeding or at the very least to lay fewer eggs. There are records of widespread death of birds under these conditions. When favorable conditions return, birds may respond by increasing their clutch size and having several generations, one after another.

Whereas most Northern Hemisphere birds enter breeding condition as a response to increasing day length, there is evidence that many Australian birds are able to become reproductive rather quickly after favorable rains have occurred. Another adaptation we have mentioned earlier: nomadism. That is, birds such as budgerigars, many other parrots, and in fact a considerable numbers of species move about to take advantage of areas where rain has fallen or where seasonal flowers or fruits are available. Even the flightless emu has been recorded as moving hundreds of miles to more favorable habitat.

Spring migrations, so characteristic of American birds, seem a good deal less marked in Australia, doubtless because severe winters occur only in parts of the highlands of the Southeast and Tasmania. According to Allen Keast, former curator of birds at the Australian Museum in Sydney, only about 8 percent of land-bird species can be considered north-south migrants, while 26 percent are nomadic and 66 percent pretty much sedentary. Much remains to be learned about the movements of birds in Australia.

One of the problems is that the rural population of humans is so sparse that recoveries of banded birds are quite infrequent.

These remarks apply only to the land birds. So far we have said nothing about water birds, which are quite a different story. We have ignored water birds not because they are not interesting, but because most of them belong to widespread, familiar groups: Australia has its share of gulls, terns, ducks, geese, herons, plovers, and the like. Some are common enough, even in cities. It is not unusual to see flocks of ibis in city parks, probing the ground for insects with their long, curved beaks.

For a time we had to walk across a soccer field in Brisbane to catch a bus each morning, and each morning we were "dive-bombed" by a pair of spur-winged plovers that were guarding the fledglings they had reared along the edge of the field. The Australian pelican is a large and handsome representative of its kind. Then, of course, there is the elegant black swan, the state bird of Western Australia, but often seen in many parts of the country. As Colin MacInnes says: "... that Australia should produce *black* swans is symptomatic of her attitude to birds: only the unusual will do."

Some sea birds are essentially nomadic, like the wandering albatross, while others have well-defined migration routes. The short-tailed shearwater, for example, breeds in burrows in the sand in Victoria and Tasmania, but during the Australian winter flies north to Japan and the Aleutians, then down through the eastern Pacific and back to Australia, even, frequently, to the very same burrow. Dominic Serventy, of the Commonwealth Scientific and Industrial Research Organization, has banded nearly 100,000 shearwaters, and even though fewer than one percent have been recovered, more is known about this species than about most sea birds.

We have not encountered the short-tailed shearwater in our travels, but on Heron Island another species, the wedge-tailed shearwater, was much in evidence. As night falls, these birds return from their fishing trips at sea, making awkward "crash landings" that sometimes seem to stun them for a moment. Then each walks to its burrow in the sand, where its partner is brooding the single egg. Each parent spends a week or two in the burrow while the other spends the days at sea; then they switch roles, until the egg hatches in about seven weeks. While the parents are together at night in the burrow, they "sing" to each other with eerie moanings and screechings, all too familiar to the tourist population of Heron Island. Just before dawn, the "off duty" parent returns to the sea. When the chick hatches, both parents feed it with regurgitated fish until it becomes very fat, when it is left to "slim down" and make its way to the sea on its own.

Both kinds of shearwaters have earned the name "mutton birds," since the fat young birds have been exploited as food. Evidently, some of the early sealers first discovered their supposedly muttonlike flavor. Harvesting these birds has become a small-scale industry, especially on the islands off Tasmania. The birds are plucked for their down, which fills many Australian sleeping bags; the oil from their innards is used in suntan lotion; while the birds themselves are sold on the market either fresh, frozen, or salted. During some years half a million mutton birds are harvested, yet the total population is so large that the species still thrives. Perhaps their main threat is not from the muttonbirders but from possible oil spills from offshore wells being built not far from their breeding grounds.

We wish there were space to tell of some of the other birds that have intrigued us. On our trip to the East Alligator Rivers in the Northern Territory, we saw water holes teeming with countless thousands of birds, including brolgas (the Australian equivalent of the whooping crane) and an occasional jabiru, a stately black-and-white, red-legged stork. Above all, magpie geese crowded the water holes by the thousands: boldly marked black-and-white geese with a caplike knob on top of their heads. Once these geese occurred widely in Australia, but their appetite for grain crops resulted in their being banished to the Far North. Much of their present range is now included in Kakadu National Park, where presumably they will continue to thrive without further conflict with man.

On a spring hike near Brisbane we found ourselves surrounded by spotted pardalotes, tiny, almost tailless birds of friendly disposition. Deep in the Outback we puzzled over the whereabouts of crested bellbirds, remarkable ventriloquists whose Morse-code–like song seems to come from where the bird isn't. We have watched the fairy penguins waddle ashore just after dark on Phillip Island, Victoria—unmindful of the floodlights and hundreds of tourists lured to the popular "penguin parade."

We have not even mentioned the majestic wedge-tailed eagle, a much persecuted bird that we nevertheless saw in some abundance en route from Alice Springs to Ayers Rock in the Center. This is one of the largest of the world's eagles, colored much like our golden eagle but having a characteristically shaped tail. The white-breasted sea eagle is also a not uncommon sight along the coast—such an elegant aeronaut that it is difficult to remember that he is a predator and a scavenger. Kites, rather slender, hawk-like carrion feeders, abound in many areas, taking the place filled by vultures in North America. By night, there is the boobook owl and the tawny frogmouth. ...

But we must stop; it is easy to become carried away on the subject of birds. On our several trips to Australia we have seen only a fraction of the species occurring there—but enough to enrich our days immeasurably.

15

An Entomologist's World-View, 1993

When Lyons and Burford agreed to republish Life on a Little-Known Planet *in 1993, I attempted to update the book a bit by adding an Epilogue. More had happened in 25 years than I could have reviewed in a few pages. In some ways it was a different world. A billion more people had been added to an already overcrowded planet, and at the same time a greater awareness had arisen concerning the loss of species, the degradation of soils, and the accumulation of wastes of all kinds. But only among a few; the rest continued to bumble on, grasping quick pleasures and hoping for true happiness in another world.*

SINCE *LIFE ON A LITTLE-KNOWN PLANET* was written in 1968, I have moved from a home in eastern suburbs to one on a rocky crag in Colorado. My neighbors are mule deer, coyotes, and an occasional black bear; mountain chickadees, Steller's jays, now and then a golden eagle. From my desk I can see parts of Rocky Mountain National Park, Comanche Peak Wilderness, and the valley of a Wild and Scenic River. I confess that I have fled in some degree of terror from the cluttered and greed-driven life of the late twentieth century. The winters here are long and cold, filled with wood-splitting, snow-shoveling, and reflection. The short summers are filled with insects, also good neighbors. Many of them have been little studied in a country that has been settled by persons of scientific bent for only a few decades. So my penchant for inquiring into insects' lives is well satisfied.

A good deal has happened since 1968 in the relationships of people to insects—indeed to the environment as a whole. The first Earth Day was held in 1970, also the year of the founding of the Environmental Protection Agency (EPA), committed (among other things) to oversee the regulation of pesticides. Some say the "era of ecology" began in the decade of the 60s, but of course there were warnings of danger to our planet long before that, for example in Aldo Leopold's 1949 *Sand County Almanac*, and even much earlier, in George Perkins Marsh's 1864 *Man and Nature*.

Once the nation's conscience had been awakened, there were many responses from Congress, for example the Toxic Substances Control Act of 1986, which curiously acquired as an acronym the name of an opera involving stabbing and death by a firing squad, but no poisoning (TOSCA). Others included the Endangered Species Act, the Wild and Scenic Rivers Act, the Clean Air Act, and various wilderness bills. Meanwhile the Food and Drug Administration (FDA) established standards for permissible levels of toxic chemicals in foods, while the Occupational Safety and Health Administration (OSHA) required worker protection from hazardous materials. Environmental organizations flourished as never before. In 1989 *Time* magazine's "Man of the Year" was "The Endangered Earth," and the cover featured a view of the earth from space. In 1992 Senator (later Vice President) Al Gore's book *Earth in the Balance* became a best seller.

In June, 1992, leaders of most countries met in Rio de Janeiro for the United Nations Conference on Environment and Development, the "Earth Summit." Besides formal speeches and meetings, there were songs, dances, and art work celebrating the environment, and a "Tree of Life" was decorated by children from all over the world. Out of the conference came a new awareness of the importance of protecting our planet from overdevelopment as well as promises to control contaminants and "greenhouse gases" (chiefly carbon dioxide) and to respect forests for their role in absorbing carbon dioxide and in providing living spaces for so many organisms. Unfortunately the United States was unwilling to support many of the proposals and could scarcely make a case for preserving tropical forests while its own forests were being so rapidly decimated.

Nevertheless the "era of ecology" is a reality, and we can be sure it is more than a fad. The "Green Revolution" of the 1960s and 70s permitted a spectacular increase in world population but at the expense of the overuse of pesticides, fertilizers, and water; more extensive monocultures; and a greater dependence on mechanized farming techniques suited to large-scale farmers and corporations. Gore believes that we need a second Green Revolution that will encourage small farmers who will use environmentally sound practices. Rather than boosting the SDI (Strategic Defense Initiative), he proposes an SEI (Strategic Environmental Initiative), which would involve, among other things, much less dependence upon insecticides and herbicides.

It is true that the use of DDT has been banned in the United States, though it is still manufactured for export. At present we produce pesticides in much greater volume than we did when *Silent Spring* was published. According to Cornell University entomologist David Pimentel, in the United States approximately 500,000 tons of 600 different kinds of pesticides are used annually at a cost of $4.1 billion. Worldwide, 2.5 million tons are applied each year at a purchase price of $20 billion.

To an ecologically conscious world, these figures seem shocking, but they are only part of the price paid to maintain agricultural food production sufficient to feed a burgeoning world population (more or less—one in ten suffers from serious malnutrition). Other costs, Pimentel points out, include human poisonings by pesticides, with as many as 20,000 deaths in the world each year (according to the World Health Organization), as well as poisoning to animals, both wild and domestic. The widespread destruction of beneficial insects has rendered them less available as natural controls and has also led to outbreaks of "secondary pests," that is, insects that do insignificant damage until an insecticide applied for another species kills off their natural enemies. Meanwhile over 500 insect and mite species have developed resistance to diverse insecticides, forcing chemical companies continually to develop and market new chemicals and entomologists to search for ways to attack pests without overloading the environment with toxins.

Unfortunately new pests appear on the scene periodically, largely a result of the fact that we now live in a world economy, where agricultural and other products are being shipped quickly all over the world. In March, 1986, an aphid (or plant louse) new to the United States was discovered on grains in Texas. With remarkable speed it spread through the wheat-growing regions of the West. By the end of 1986 it was already reported from most of the states of the Great Plains, and by 1990 it had reached California, Washington, and three provinces of Canada. Wheat and barley plants infested with the aphid were stunted, and leaf blades streaked and curled around groups of feeding aphids. Crop losses in 1990 exceeded $30 million. A series of conferences were convened to address this new and unexpected threat to America's breadbasket. Despite prompt response by federal and state authorities, the aphid remains a major pest.

Arrival of the aphid in Texas was first spotted by a county agent, who had the foresight to send specimens to the Systematic Entomology Laboratory of the U.S. Department of Agriculture, in Beltsville, Maryland. Here the aphid specialist, Manya Stoetzel, identified the species, making it possible to trace its origin and past history. It was discovered that it had been noted devastating grains in Russia in the late 1800s, and the Russians had worked out its natural history and made suggestions for its control as early as 1914. Russians called it the barley aphid, but in America it has come to be called the Russian wheat aphid. From Russia it spread to the Mediterranean area, then in 1978 to South Africa, where it became a serious pest. In 1980 it was first noticed in Mexico, from which it spread in a few years all the way to Canada.

The aphids are less than an eighth of an inch long, but they have remarkable powers of reproduction. Without the distractions of sex, females give birth to a series of aphidlets, which in a few weeks grow up to produce still more. Males have never been found in North America, though they are reported from Russia. Twice a year, a generation of winged individuals is produced, and with the aid of wind currents they disperse widely to new fields. Other generations are wingless, moving about little and gorging on plant sap. Wild grasses serve as food sources when wheat or barley are not available. Entomologists promptly designed an emergency program for the Russian wheat aphid, recommending pesticides with forbidding names such as chlorpyrifos and disulfoton. Long-range plans call for the development of strains resistant to the aphids and the introduction of natural enemies. After the investment of a great many tax dollars, progress is being made toward learning to live with this unwelcome immigrant.

As if this were not enough, in 1991 crops in California's Imperial Valley were devastated by a "superbug" that in a single year caused a reduction in crop yield valued at $200 million and caused Governor Pete Wilson to declare a state of emergency in the Valley. Yet this "superbug" was even smaller than the Russian wheat aphid, less than a tenth of an inch long, a whitefly not unlike those that householders and greenhouse operators find forming white specks on their plants. Whiteflies are not true flies, but sucking insects related to aphids. They make up for their small size by their reproductive capacities and their ability to transmit several plant diseases. The whitefly first appeared on poinsettias in Florida in 1986, but it soon appeared in other parts of the South, probably from poinsettias shipped about the country in the Christmas trade. Among the crops in the diet of this minute insect are melons, lettuce, broccoli, alfalfa, cotton, corn, tomatoes, and peanuts. A California entomologist reported that a field that usually yielded 750,000 melons produced only 50 in 1991.

By 1992 the whiteflies were causing alarm throughout the South, and had spread north into California's rich San Joaquin Valley. It was estimated that 10,000 jobs had been lost, chiefly to migrant workers. Although the whiteflies look exactly like sweet-potato whiteflies, which have been in the United States since 1894, researchers began to suspect they must represent a species newly introduced into the country. Using the recently developed technique of isoelectric focusing, they discovered that the new pests have quite a different profile of enzymes. So they now consider it a previously unrecognized species, which they call the silverleaf whitefly after a silvering of the leaves of squash resulting from their feeding.

Whiteflies are notoriously difficult to control, as they aggregate on the undersides of leaves, where they escape most sprays. Also, whiteflies readily develop resistance to insecticides. The best opportunities may lie in biological control. A parasitic wasp that was used some years ago to control the ash whitefly nearly wiped out that pest, but it may not work for the silverleaf whitefly. These wasps lay their eggs inside the whitefly larva, so they are extremely minute. Since no one is sure where the silverleaf whitefly came from originally, it may be difficult to locate a natural enemy that is specifically adapted to that species.

Faced with continuing and often unexpected outbreaks of agricultural pests, and with an increasing public awareness of the danger of drenching the earth with pesticides, entomologists are developing some quite different approaches to problem-solving. It is no longer fashionable to speak of "control" of pests, but rather of "management," in recognition of the fact that accomplishments must always be balanced against costs, both financial and ecological. It is a multifaceted approach in which such things as timing of plowing, planting, and harvesting, natural enemies, insect pathogens, resistant strains of plants, and other possibilities are carefully considered. When synthetic pesticides must be applied, as they still often must be, efforts must be made to apply them when they will not conflict with other measures and to use chemicals that have little or no toxicity to humans or animals. Control of plant diseases and weeds may also have to be integrated with that of insects. Entomologists gather data and develop a unified program to manage each pest problem as it arises, using the acronym IPM (which can stand for either integrated pest management or insect pest management). Although the concept of IPM goes back at least to the 1960s, only in the last two decades has it become the touchstone of entomological practice. Still more recently, those concerned with plant protection have favored a more euphemistic phrase: plant health care (PHC).

Whether one calls it IPM or PHC (we live in an age of acronyms!) the first step requires an evaluation of the problem, often involving standardized sampling methods to determine population levels of the pest and its natural enemies. Plant damage may prove to have a different cause, perhaps a nutritional deficiency, a disease, or a drifting herbicide. If it is determined that an insect problem exists, various alternatives are considered, to be used separately or in concert. Will the value of the crop justify the costs of containment? We are now so used to perfect (and very expensive) apples, for example, that a rigorous program of control can be justified. (But do we really need perfect apples, each carefully polished and individually labeled?)

It is easy to overreact to a problem that is not serious or is self-correcting. Plants often recover from insect attack, and may even increase photosynthesis following insect feeding. Outbreaks of forest pests tend to occur periodically and to decline in three or four years as insect diseases and parasitic insects increase in number. Foresters and recreationists often become alarmed by such outbreaks. In 1973 an outbreak of Douglas-fir tussock moth larvae in the Far West resulted in defoliation of over 700,000 acres of timber. Alarm was such that a bill was introduced into Congress to permit the use of DDT, which had been banned from general use a year earlier. When aerial dusting was employed, the tussock moths were already in decline, and it is possible that dusting actually prolonged the outbreak by killing off natural enemies. In retrospect, some concluded that the moths may have done as much long-range good as short-term harm. Drastic disturbances in forests may be required periodically to improve diversity and to increase the availability of nutrients (for example, from nitrogen-rich insect droppings) and to provide light and space for the growth of new trees.

My very first job, way back in 1941, involved the dissemination of the spores of a bacterium, *Bacillus popillae*, in New England lawns and golf courses. The bacterium produces a "milky disease" of the grubs of Japanese beetles which had gradually caused a substantial reduction in populations of that pest. In recent years a bacterial wilt disease of leaf-feeding insects has attracted much attention. It can be disseminated much like a pesticide and even combined with a chemical pesticide. The bacterium in this case is *Bacillus thuringiensis*, named for a German city, Thuringen, where it was first discovered. More often it is referred to by its abbreviation, Bt. Many strains of Bt are now known, each with a specificity for a certain group of insects. The spores are resistant to heat and dryness, and during spore formation crystals highly toxic to insects are formed. A number of companies now produce products based on Bt, under a variety of names. Insects that have been successfully controlled include the Colorado potato beetle and caterpillars such as the imported cabbageworm and the gypsy moth.

It is generally agreed that Bt poses no threat to people or to the environment. It has also proved possible to insert genetically engineered Bt toxins into plants. Such transgenic plants have been produced experimentally for tobacco, cotton, tomatoes, and potatoes. The plants are protected against certain insect pests that feed on them, and may soon be available to farmers. Some molecular biologists envisage a day when traditional insecticides will be replaced by genetically engineered crops which will automatically repel or kill insects that feed on them. This raises a problem: is a tomato that contains genes that produce Bt toxins or feeding deterrents derived from another plant still a tomato? Or must it be registered as an insecticide?

This may prove to be a moot question, as there is growing evidence that many insects are developing resistance to Bt and may well develop resistance to transgenic plants containing Bt toxins. This is perhaps not surprising, considering the ability of insects to evolve rapidly, via natural selection, in the presence of so many causes of mortality. There is evidence that insects may sometimes evolve novel life cycles that subvert our efforts to control them. For many years crop rotation was used to reduce populations of corn rootworms (larvae of a small, attractive leaf beetle). Since the rootworms have a one-year life cycle and feed only on corn, farmers who alternate corn with soybeans or small grains on an annual basis cause the rootworms to die off or emigrate for lack of food. But at least some populations of the beetles have evolved the ability to produce eggs that undergo a long resting stage, producing larvae during a second season, when the unwary farmer has once again planted corn.

Throughout the centuries many plants have evolved chemical defenses against insect feeding, keeping "one jump ahead" of insects' ability to overcome them. Some of the "botanical insecticides" were in use well before there were people who called themselves entomologists. Pyrethrum, derived from flowers of *Chrysanthemum*, was used in Asia for the control of lice and fleas several centuries ago and it is still used for the quick knock-down of many insects while having little effect on mammals. Rotenone, derived from the roots of several tropical plants, also has a long history of use to kill insects, with little or no toxicity for warm-blooded animals. Nicotine, derived from tobacco and related plants, is still another, though much more poisonous to people and animals. Abamectin, derived from a soil fungus, has recently been used effectively against fire ants and several other pests. There are many other substances produced by plants to repel insects that await evaluations as insecticides.

In recent years, there has been much interest in a tree of the Far East called the neem tree. An extract of the seed pods called azadirachtin is a potent insecticide with low toxicity to people, animals, or plants. The poison apparently acts as a growth inhibitor, perhaps because it mimics the insects' own growth hormones. Insects are unable to molt properly and wither away before reaching maturity. So neem extract acts rather slowly, and as of now it is expensive and has been used primarily on ornamental plants.

The neem tree has many other qualities. Compounds from the seeds and leaves have antiseptic action and show promise as contraceptives. Neem oil has been used for soaps and lubricants, and the trees provide shade and lumber. Farmers in "third world" countries can grow their own neem trees and acquire many benefits from this "wonder tree." Native to India and Burma, the tree is now grown in Africa, the Caribbean, and in parts of Florida, California, and Hawaii.

Other insect growth regulators (IGRs) besides neem extract have been discovered or synthesized. Several are now commercially available, some of them disrupting molting and others interfering with cuticle formation. Although they are slow-acting and must strike at a critical stage in the life cycle, they are beginning to play a role in the control of insects that have developed resistance to most insecticides, such as the California floodwater mosquito.

We now know that insects produce many chemicals that they use in their own defense against predators or in communication with other members of their own species. Those used in communication are called pheromones. Traps baited with pheromones of a particular species (such as the gypsy moth or the Mediterranean fruit fly) have been effective in determining whether the species is present in a given area or plentiful enough to be of concern. Introduction of synthetic sex pheromone in small tubes or microcapsules spread over cotton fields by helicopters often results in the disruption of the mating of pink bollworm moths to the extent that the use of conventional insecticides can be greatly reduced.

Wendell Roelofs and his colleagues at Cornell University have identified the sex pheromone of the grape berry moth and dispersed it on the supporting wires in vineyards in the form of small "twisties" similar to those used to close garbage bags. Under experimental conditions, mating was disrupted to the extent that damage to the grapes was below 1 percent, as compared to two plots treated with insecticide, where damage was 2.5 percent and 18 percent. Since vineyards are often close to residences, pheromones seem to provide an ideal method of suppressing populations of the berry moth.

Warehouse managers and food processors often use pheromone-baited traps to discover infestations by weevils, flour moths, and other pests of foodstuffs, since insect fragments in foods may cause them to be condemned. When insect populations are not too high, mass trapping can sometimes eliminate the pests. In at least one case, it proved possible to attract males to a pheromone-baited trap containing spores of a disease organism, which were then carried to the females when they mated.

Pheromones of over 450 insect species have now been identified; many have been synthesized and quite a few are commercially available. There has been some resistance to their use: farmers like to see insects dead, not simply confused, and chemical companies would rather produce and market pesticides that can be used to kill a variety of species, not just one. Pheromones also have the disadvantage of being highly volatile; if they were not it would hardly serve their function in communication. On the other hand, it seems unlikely that insects will ever develop resistance to substances that they themselves produce. Or will they evolve new forms of sex pheromone molecules if we continue to harass them? "*Ils sont capables de tout*," wrote a French entomologist. It is possible to believe anything of insects.

Organic gardening has become increasingly popular in the United States, and many small farmers in other parts of the world have always farmed organically. Universal organic farming may not be a practicable way to feed the world's exploding population, but there is growing faith in what is often called alternative agriculture. The term applies to any system of food or fiber production that makes use of natural processes such as predators and parasites, crop rotation to mitigate pest problems and increase soil nutrients, use of genetically improved crops, and other environmentally healthy and often relatively inexpensive procedures. Pesticides are used under IPM programs while less drastic methods of pest containment are being developed. The recent volume *Alternative Agriculture*, produced by the National Research Council, points out that federal policies often work against such practices, placing high priority on uniformity of crops that meet standards that have little relation to nutritional quality. Many growers are enrolled in federal crop commodity programs that discourage diversity or the departure from standardized procedures. Pheromones, oddly, must be registered with the EPA as pesticides, even though they are species-specific and pose no threat to the environment or to people. A tedious, expensive, and time-consuming procedure is required before pheromones can be registered for use.

As of today, the production of blemish-free fruits and vegetables that meet federal standards and justify higher prices often requires the use of pesticides on a regularly scheduled basis. The planting of monocultures of genetically uniform crops greatly increases the risk of attack by novel pests such as the Russian wheat aphid and the silverleaf whitefly. Figures for 1986 show that for most crops, less than half the current acreage is grown under IPM regimens. Use of IPM does not necessarily mean fewer pesticide applications; sometimes field scouting and cost-benefit analysis result in more pesticide use. But in most cases the reverse is true. Any diminution in the amount of toxic chemicals applied to the land must be welcomed.

Seen in a broader context, the overuse of pesticides is only one of many threats to the world environment, and perhaps a minor one compared to our inability to find places to dispose of all our household, industrial, and nuclear wastes—and especially our inability to check population growth and the concomitant loss of habitat for wildlife and of quality living space for people. Threats of global warming and of loss of the protective layer of ozone in the atmosphere also loom large. But perhaps the most frightening of immediate crises is the apparent inability of humans to live amicably together, without rancor towards others of different skin color, beliefs, or life styles. Three members of the Project on Environmental Change and Acute Conflict, writing in *Scientific American*, make a convincing case that scarcities of renewable resources are significantly contributing to conflicts in many parts of the world, foreshadowing a surge of similar violence in the future. Among other things, the amount of available crop land and of water per person is certain to decrease dramatically in the next few decades, triggering further clashes and displacement of populations.

Over 1,600 scientists from many countries have recently signed a "Warning to Humanity" (it has so far been largely ignored by the press, which would rather not rile its advertisers). "Human beings and the natural world are on a collision course," reads the warning. Critical stresses to the atmosphere, soils, oceans, fresh water, forests, and species are discussed, and of course the overriding specter of unrestrained population growth with its accompanying conversion of resources into wastes.

Battle lines have been drawn, for there are many unwilling to accept this wholly new and inconvenient mind-set. In the West, where I live, a group called the Wise Use Movement (WUM) makes a point of challenging environmentalists both in print and at meetings where the use of land is under discussion. It is supported by mining and logging corporations, and to some extent by farmers and ranchers, and its financial backing far exceeds that of those whom they call "tree huggers," or much worse. The spotted owl, the desert pup-fish, wolves and grizzlies, cannot be allowed to interfere with what they consider their "God-given" right to use the land for whatever dollars they can wring from it.

In the make-believe world of tinsel and television in which we spend most of our hours, it is easy to forget that our dependence upon the environment in its broadest sense—including climate, soils, plants, and animals—remains total, and that we are far from understanding it fully. In our hectic lives it is easy, too, to forget that there is (at least we hope) a future, and that it is our children and grandchildren who will experience it. Should we not be embracing the environment rather than trashing it; should we not be exploring it deeply, learning what it may have to teach us about living on earth in concert with ourselves and our surroundings? Can we be complacent when we hear that species extinction is estimated to be 27,000 a year, or three every hour?

Persons who doubt these figures on species extinction, or their importance, are invited to read Edward O. Wilson's 1992 book *The Diversity of Life.* In fact these are conservative estimates. More than half of all species may still be unknown to science, and many are doubtless being eliminated by habitat destruction before we salute their presence. A great many of these still unknown species occur in the deep sea and in tropical rain forests, but by no means all—last year I collected a species of wasp new to science on the deck of my house. How many potential new drugs and new foods are we forfeiting through ignorance and callousness; how many potential environment-friendly pesticides; how many petroleum or rubber substitutes, or sources of fiber, spices, condiments; how much beauty, excitement, inspiration?

16

Remembering Pioneer Naturalists

In 1986 Antaeus *devoted an issue to a collection of nature writings, to which I was asked to contribute. A year later it appeared in book form, edited by Daniel Halpern and published by North Point Press. I lifted parts of this essay for inclusion in my book* Pioneer Naturalists: The Discovery and Naming of North American Plants and Animals *(Henry Holt, 1993).*

A FEW YEARS AGO we decided to spend our declining years in a habitat of our choice, far from the screech of traffic, the aromas of industry, and the too-visible signs of what passes for progress. We had, after all, done our small bit for society, trying to instill in our students and our children something of the reverence we have always felt for that delicate and incredibly complex earthly wrapping called the biosphere. Now we wished to indulge in a final orgy of what Edward Wilson has called biophilia—more than a love, an *affiliation* with life in its broadest sense. There are others, of course, who have "moved to the woods," seeking like Thoreau to become inspectors of rainstorms and surveyors of forest paths. We selected a granite cliff in the Colorado Rockies, with a view across meadows and valleys to the Mummy Range, cresting at over 13,000 feet elevation. The area is called Glacier View Meadows, though the best it can claim is a distant view of a few semipermanent snow fields. We were greedy for as big a piece of the biosphere as we could absorb from our windows—fifty miles, more or less, to the south and east, and (from nearby promontories) nearly as far to the north and west.

But more than living among rocks and chipmunks, we wished to relive some of the discoveries of the things around us. Outside, a Cassin's finch is busy at our feeder; a Cooper's hawk traverses the valley below; Abert's squirrels gambol on the rocks; in the spring the hillsides will sparkle with *Claytonia* (spring beauties); the valleys will ring with the songs of Wilson's warblers and the woods with the drumming of Williamson's sapsuckers. Cassin, Cooper, Abert, Clayton, Wilson, Williamson, and so many more: though long gone they live by having had their names attached to species that survive—and will survive, we hope, for a very long time. Their discoveries were made at a time when life in the wild was not easy, and some gave their lives in the search for a fuller knowledge of living things. They deserve to be remembered, and we resolve to remember them.

Now, as I write this in winter, the world is stripped of much of its vitality. Rocks, snow, pines, dead herbs and grasses whipped by a bitter wind. But still those most elegant of birds are about, the Steller's jays: breast and tail blue as the late evening sky, back and head like the night sky, white streaks about their eyes giving them a roguish appearance that suits them well. Their crests are the longest of any of our birds, composed of feathers that can be erected or depressed to suit their moods. Unfortunately they are not musicians, but they do at least produce an interesting variety of sounds, some of them resembling the calls of red-tailed hawks. In summer they eat a great many insects, but the benefits they perform are outweighed by their appetite for the eggs of other birds. In the winter they supplement a diet of pine seeds with whatever scraps they can find, and they are regular visitors to our feeders. So adaptable are they that they thrive all the way from Alaska to Guatemala, but always in forested mountain country. Ornithologist Elliott Coues described them well: "a tough, wiry, independent creature, with sense enough to take precious good care of himself."

Out our window, last fall, we saw a sharp-shinned hawk trying to catch a Steller's jay in a Douglas fir. The jay hopped about where the branches were thickest, rather than taking wing, where it surely would have been caught. The hawk left without a meal.

The jays are named for Georg Wilhelm Steller, who first discovered them in 1741. Steller was a German naturalist who was attached to a Russian expedition that left Kamchatka in two ships to explore the "Great Land" to the east, now called Alaska. It was headed by Vitus Bering (a Dane), for whom the Bering Sea is named. Steller discovered not only the jays but several other creatures that were later named for him: Steller's sea-eagle, Steller's eider duck, and Steller's sea cow (now extinct). He found the jays during a landfall on Kayak Island (not far from present-day Valdez). He recognized them at once as relatives of the blue jays of eastern North America, which had been described a few years earlier. "This bird [he said] proved to me that we were really in America."

In fact Steller was able to spend only one day on the Alaska coast before Bering set sail for home. But they were busy hours, and resulted in the first scientific report on the plants and animals of Alaska. In the words of a biographer, "perhaps no other naturalist in history ever accomplished so monumental a task under such difficulties and in so little time." The return trip proved disastrous. Violent storms constantly drove the ships off course, and it was late November before they approached the Asiatic continent. In fact they did not make it, for they were shipwrecked on what is now called Bering Island. Bering died there, and most of the officers and crew were ill with scurvy. Remarkably, Steller and several others built a new ship from the remains of the old. They arrived safely in Kamchatka the following summer. But Steller was plagued with bad luck and died a few years later while wandering around Siberia, still finding plants and animals new to science. Fortunately his journals survived, so we may still share in his adventures. It is good to be reminded of him by so visible a bird.

Douglas firs dominate the view from three of the four sides of our house: stately, symmetrical trees, hung with shaggy cones, in winter decorated with globs of snow. To be sure, those that grow along the semiarid slopes of the Front Range cannot rival those of the humid Northwest. David Douglas, exploring Oregon Territory in 1825, was awed by these great trees; one that he measured was 227 feet tall and 48 feet in circumference. Our trees do not exceed 50 feet in height, though some in nearby ravines surpass 100. Douglas firs range all the way from British Columbia to northern Mexico, from sea level to (in the southern Rockies) over 10,000 feet, and from places with only 20 inches annual rainfall to places with well over 100. It would be difficult to find another tree adapted to such a broad range of circumstances. Douglas firs are tough in other ways. Over two hundred kinds of insects are known to attack them. Some of these are very destructive locally, particularly western spruce budworms and Douglas fir beetles. Some trees are killed, but others spring up to take their places. These are relatively fast-growing trees, but when well established they may live several hundred years.

Douglas firs are not really true firs, nor are they spruces, though they look superficially like both. The cones are very different: they are pendant, with bracts extending from between the scales. Each bract has a double end with a slender filament between: rather like the tail ends of tiny animals plunging into the cones to escape a hawk circling overhead. The scientific name, *Pseudotsuga taxifolia* (false hemlock with yew leaves!), reveals the puzzle the trees presented to early taxonomists. [Currently, the name *Pseudotsuga menziesii* is applied to the trees.] In the Northwest, these are timber trees of major importance; in fact they surpass all other tree species in the value of lumber produced. No one is likely to eye our trees for lumber. But as fuel, Douglas fir, along with ponderosa pine, keeps us twice warm, as the saying goes: once in the splitting and once in the burning.

David Douglas was not the first to discover the trees, but he was the first to send living material back to England, where the trees became important ornamentals. Douglas was born to a poor family in Scone, Scotland, in 1799. He was apprenticed as a youth to a gardener and showed so much talent that by the time he was 24 he had been hired by the Royal Horticultural Society of London as a field collector. The Society was actively involved in importing plants from many parts of the world to enrich British gardens.

Douglas's first trip was to New York and Ontario, with a side trip to Philadelphia, where he met Thomas Nuttall. On the next trip the Horticultural Society sent him, via Cape Horn, to join the Hudson's Bay Company's outposts on the Columbia River. As he roamed about the Northwest, and later California, he met with a variety of misadventures, but in spite of problems he collected specimens, seeds, and roots of many plants new to science. He was the discoverer of some of the Far West's most distinctive trees: sugar pine, western white pine, silver fir, Oregon white oak, and several others. The Northwest was then a land of dense forests and giant trees, peopled by Indians and by transplanted Europeans mainly involved in the fur trade. Douglas was a complex person, troubled by indecision and the fear of failure. One of his shortcomings was an inability to estimate altitudes. While crossing the Rockies, Douglas climbed Mt. Brown, which he thought to be about 16,000 feet, highest in the Rockies. It is now known to be 9,156 feet in elevation!

In a fit of pique, in 1833 Douglas resigned from the Horticultural Society and traveled to Hawaii where, at the age of thirty-four, he fell into a trap set to capture wild cattle and was trampled to death by a bull—a dismal end of a person said to have had more plants named in his honor than anyone else in the history of botany.

Now and then, quite unpredictably, Clark's nutcrackers appear around our home in numbers, calling each other harshly from treetops. These are large, striking birds, mostly light gray but with black wings and tail broadly banded with white. Most of the time they live high in the mountains, close to treeline, but at times they seem afflicted with wanderlust and roam far from their breeding sites. Along Trail Ridge Road in Rocky Mountain National Park they can often be seen taking snacks from the tourists. Their usual food is pine seeds, which they collect by hammering the cones apart with their powerful beaks. They breed very early in the season, often laying their eggs in March. Females have been seen incubating their eggs in snowstorms, with the temperature close to zero.

When pine seeds are ripe in the fall, nutcrackers collect them in great quantity and cache them for recovery during the winter and spring. The seeds are buried an inch or two deep, usually on cliff ledges or south-facing slopes. A single nutcracker may store as many as 50,000 pine seeds. Since they put only a few seeds in a cache, each bird must remember several thousand hiding places. Evidently they memorize large landmarks in the area as well as small landmarks close to the caches. They have been seen uncovering caches under several feet of snow. It is estimated that it takes about ten thousand seeds to support a nutcracker from October to April—to say nothing of what may be required to feed the young. Even so, they bury many more seeds than they need; they must compensate for a considerable loss to rodents. When recovering seeds, they land at a selected spot, probe with their bill, then dig with sideswiping motions of the bill. When seeds are found, they are cracked open at the site and eaten or carried back to the nest in a pouch beneath the tongue.

These unusual birds were fittingly named for a remarkable man: William Clark. He and Meriwether Lewis became acquainted during the Indian wars, when they both served under "Mad Anthony" Wayne. When Thomas Jefferson purchased Louisiana Territory from Napoleon in 1803, he selected these two to head an expedition with the object of "exploring the Missouri and whatever river, heading into that, leads to the western ocean." Neither Lewis nor Clark had much formal education, but Jefferson arranged for a "crash course" in botany, zoology, medicine, and navigation for Lewis, then his secretary. In the course of the expedition, now a classic of American history, Clark quickly learned to be a superb geographer as well as an accurate observer of the environment through which he passed. His and Lewis's descriptions of the plants and animals they saw and collected were often so detailed that they can be easily recognized. However, it remained for other, better trained biologists to supply formal names and descriptions for the plants and animals they recorded. In his book *Lewis and Clark: Pioneer Naturalists*, Paul Russell Cutright has dutifully compiled a list of the biological discoveries of the expedition, covering forty-seven pages and including many species that were named for the two leaders.

It was on August 22, 1804, while crossing what is now Idaho, that Clark noted "a Bird of the woodpecker kind which fed on Pine burs. Its Bill and tale white the wings black ... about the size of a robin." That he called it a woodpecker is not surprising, since the flight is undulating and the huge bill suggestive of a woodpecker. Specimens were collected and eventually found their way to pioneer ornithologist Alexander Wilson, who figured the bird in his *American Ornithology* in 1811, appropriately on the same plate with Lewis's woodpecker. Wilson called it "Clark's crow," a more suitable name since it is a member of the crow family.

It would take many pages to do justice to the discoveries of the Lewis and Clark expedition. Two genera of plants were named for them: *Lewisia* became the generic name of the bitterroot, or rock rose, the roots of which served the Indians as food (now the state flower of Montana); *Clarkia* came to be applied to another showy, pink flower, often called ragged robin (a member of the evening primrose family). Lewis was the first to discover the poorwill, a bird that calls from the valley below our house on warm summer nights. He found a poorwill that appeared torpid, as if hibernating (in October, in the Dakotas). This was a novel discovery; in fact poorwills are one of the very few birds that do hibernate. But Audubon elected to name it *Caprimulgus nuttallii*, after Thomas Nuttall, a later "discoverer." Nevertheless, there are plenty of plants and animals around to remind us of Lewis and Clark—and of course Nuttall, too, is worth remembering.

To persons attuned to nature, there are few dramas more rewarding than the sequence of wildflowers that through the spring and summer spring from the ground, often in the most unlikely places. Can anything compare to the sight of the first yellow violets blooming along a woodland path? These most fragile of plants are yet hardy enough to bloom when nights are still frosty and snow still lingers in the ravines. Hereabouts, yellow violets (*Viola nuttallii*) appear in May, when (as our wildflower guide puts it) "crows are incubating, wood ducks beginning to nest." Despite their lack of odor, violets have a quiet charm and a distinctive flower shape that is theirs alone. In fact they need no odor, as they are self-fertile and have no need to attract bees. The violet's showy flowers rarely set seed; instead, inconspicuous flowers close to the ground that do not open are the ones that produce the seeds. Violets are edible plants, used by some tribes of Indians as greens and by early settlers for thickening soups or making violet tea. We may try them some day, though it seems a shame to pick such delicate plants. Violets are major food plants for the caterpillars of several of our local fritillary butterflies; perhaps we had best leave them for the butterflies.

It was Frederick Pursh who named these plants after Nuttall. Pursh had been hired to describe and name the plants collected on the Lewis and Clark Expedition, and he also had access to many of the plants collected by Nuttall. Pursh came to regard the specimens as his personal property, and he carried them off to London. Said Nuttall of him: "It was not surely honorable to snatch from me the little imaginary credit due my enthusiastic researches made at the most imminent risk of personal safety." But

Pursh got his comeuppance. Bitterbrush (*Purshia*) was named for him, as well as *Astragalus purshii* (a locoweed!).

Thomas Nuttall seems to have packed several lifetimes into one. Born in England in 1786 and devoted to natural history since childhood, he emigrated to Philadelphia when he was twenty-two and determined to spend his life exploring the plants of the New World. Although he had little training, he was employed by Dr. Benjamin Barton, author of the first American textbook of botany, to collect plants in the Northwest. Here he joined Astor's American Fur Company and traveled up the Missouri River, returning by way of New Orleans. He traveled in the wilds and was lost several times. Washington Irving said of him (in *Astoria*): "Delighted with the treasures, he went groping and stumbling along among a wilderness of sweets, forgetful of everything but his immediate pursuit. The Canadian voyageurs used to make merry at his expense, regarding him as some whimsical kind of madman."

Back in Philadelphia and disappointed that he was not asked to join Stephen Long's expedition of 1819–1820 to the Rocky Mountains, Nuttall set off on his own for the Arkansas River, where he collected many new plants despite a variety of adventures with the Indians. Soon afterward he was appointed instructor in natural history at Harvard, a position in which he flourished despite his lack of an academic background. After a decade at Harvard, he was off again to the West, this time teaming up with John Kirk Townsend and traveling all the way to the Pacific Northwest and later to California. (This was several years after Douglas's trip to these same regions.) One of his former Harvard students, Richard Henry Dana, found Nuttall on a California beach stuffing shells into his bulging pockets, an event recorded in his classic *Two Years Before the Mast.* Nuttall took passage on Dana's ship, returning east via Cape Horn. At the age of fifty-six he retired to England.

On their grand tour of the Far West, Townsend wrote of him: "Throughout the whole of our long journey, I have had constantly to admire the ardor and perfect indefatigability with which he has devoted himself to the grand object of his tour. No difficulty, no danger, no fatigue has ever daunted him."

Nuttall provided formal descriptions and names for many important plants, including western larch, Oregon ash, Rocky Mountain iris, and many others. And many were named for him besides the yellow violet. *Cornus nuttalli*, a dogwood, was named by none other than John James Audubon. Audubon was, of course, not a botanist, but in his painting of the band-tailed pigeon he included the food plant, which he named for his good friend Thomas Nuttall. A good many creatures other than plants also bear Nuttall's name: Nuttall's woodpecker, Nuttall's warbler, and of course the poorwill. As I write this a cottontail rabbit is sitting on the rocks staring in the window: *Sylvilagus nuttallii*. I can scarcely expect a more insistent reminder of a naturalist with whom I would have enjoyed a few weeks in the field—though I am sure he would have left me exhausted!

The prolonged melody of the Townsend's solitaire evokes wild mountain forests: a flute obbligato to the wind in the pines and firs. Solitaire: a word for hermit, a being that is self-sufficient and in little need of companionship. Solitaires, indeed, are rarely to be seen in flocks, and they disdain our feeders, surviving the winter perfectly well on juniper berries. Not really beautiful birds except in song: gray, with a white eye ring, a dash of buff on the wings and of white on the tail. However, the young, after they leave the nest, are striking birds, completely covered with white polka dots, as if ready for a masquerade ball. When we first saw one we rushed to our bird guide, thinking we had spotted a stray from some other continent.

In the summer, males perch on the tops of tall trees, defending their nesting territories by pouring song over the hills. These are among the few birds that sing at almost any time of year. But in the fall and early winter the songs are a bit more subdued, and in fact are produced by both males and females, which have established feeding territories where there are good sources of winter food. Male and female solitaires look alike—in contrast to their relatives the bluebirds—and along with the similarity in color goes an almost equal vocal proficiency, though the songs differ in function according to the season. Like true hermits, solitaires go their own way, individualists in every sense.

John Kirk Townsend discovered the solitaire in 1836 while trekking through Wyoming. In his journal he remarked that he had found "a beautiful new species of mocking bird." Indeed, solitaires do resemble mockingbirds in many ways, although they are thrushes. Solitaires were only one of many novelties collected by Townsend in his travels in the Northwest. Others included Townsend's warbler, Townsend's big-eared bat, Townsend's ground squirrel, and the white-tailed jackrabbit (*Lepus townsendii*). He was also the discoverer of the lark bunting, now the state bird of Colorado.

Townsend was a Philadelphia Quaker, trained in medicine but from youth fascinated by birds. When he was in his twenties he had an opportunity to join an expedition to the Columbia River, led by Nathaniel Wyeth (for whom the dwarf sunflower, *Wyethia*, was named, by Nuttall). Townsend concentrated on birds, mammals, and reptiles, while his companion Nuttall was collecting plants. Townsend's *Narrative of a Journey Across the Rocky Mountains to the Columbia River* tells of some of their adventures. He collected snakes and lizards in whisky, the only readily available preservative. But the tailor of the expedition, named Thornburg, had a great thirst for "ardent spirits." One day Townsend was away collecting, and when he returned he found that Thornburg "had decanted the liquor from the precious reptiles which I had destined for immortality, and he ... had been 'happy' upon it for a whole day." These specimens did not survive, but Townsend brought back a great many others. They were studied by (among others) Audubon, who duly included them in his monumental volumes on birds and mammals.

To be sure, a living thing is more than a name. But names are what we use to call forth the essence of what they are, and often something of the history of their discovery. "What is nature," asked Thoreau, "unless there is an eventful human like passing within her?" We enjoy our Clark's nutcrackers, our *Viola nuttalli* for themselves and as part of a vast interconnected web of living things of which we, too, are a part. We enjoy them more for having found, in their names, a clue to their initial impingement on the human endeavor. It may not matter to a Steller's jay that his kind was discovered on the Alaska coast by a German naturalist who perished a few years later in the wilds of Siberia. But to us it makes the jays that much more worthy of our attention and admiration. May they continue to thrive; and may the memory of Steller, Douglas, Townsend, and the other pioneer naturalists endure as long as there are people who find joy in their discoveries.

17

Afield in the High Country

High Country News is a biweekly newspaper, published in Paonia, Colorado, and serving as a forum for environmental problems of the western states—how to live comfortably (if that is possible) in the face of urban sprawl and threats to national parks and forests and to the native flora and fauna. Now and then they publish a column called Afield, to which I have contributed from time to time. Here are two essays, published 19 March 1984 and 6 May 1991, respectively.

A Tribute to Spring's Resurgence of Life

People have an infinite capacity for indifference and boredom, for taking even the most startling things for granted. Perhaps this is as it should be, for if we were truly caught up in the drama of the living world, we would remain in such a continual state of awe and wonderment that we would soon collapse exhausted.

Take, for example, our back yard. In winter it is a dreary place. The grass is brown, the sunflowers are bent and broken, the cottonwoods stark and somnolent. In March there is a bit of greening; in April and May there will be a resurgence of life that would be breathtaking if I were not preoccupied with more "important" things. Rightfully, I should be out there every minute, measuring each green blade, noting the progress of every bud. But I shall take it all casually, as if I will live to see a thousand springs, as if my back yard were not a place of miracles.

Still, these things do register. Even in winter, grass heads pierce the snow, causing small drifts which they embellish with swaying shadows. A rough herb stands boldly erect, defying the harsh wind. Was it a goldenrod? A fleabane?

Just a few weeks ago, as a result of a sudden drop in temperature, our local pond became a field of diamonds. The entire frozen surface was sprinkled with enormous ice crystals, many an inch or more across. Each consisted of several fernlike fronds which, as the sun passed across the sky, caught the light at various angles, producing a glitter that lasted all day. Winter may be a period of dormancy for much of the living world, but water molecules, it seems, try to fill the gap, growing meadows of crystals, jungles on windowpanes.

But these are cold and acerbic, and no bees fly among them. What a joy it was, last spring, to be studying ice crystals along a stream and suddenly to stumble upon the first pasque flowers pushing through the snow. Within a few days, the hills danced with these improbable "wild crocuses," and a few small insects were already at work on the blossoms. In shady spots, spring beauties sparkled like metamorphosed snow crystals, and in sunnier sites the sand lilies were drifted. I noted no ecstasy in the eyes of the cows that grazed there, but in their way they surely appreciated the greening of the countryside.

What a flower-filled summer it turned out to be! Tulip gentians flourished among the rank grasses in our back yard, and the foothills radiated with wallflowers. When the snows began to melt in the high country, we were there to greet the avalanche lilies, knowing they would last but a week or two.

On a fine day in August we hiked to a favorite valley, where the continental divide makes a loop to the Never Summer Range. Mountain bluebells were waist-high, delphiniums even higher. Hillsides were splashed white with bistort and yellow with composites; the trails were lined with scarlet gilia. As we approached timberline the bluebells shrank to knee height, then to ankle height, finally giving way to mats of moss campion and other diminutive flowers. But even here there were insects about the business of pollination: bees, flies, and small blue butterflies. Our camp that night was close beside a snowbank that was melting back bit by bit. Primroses were pushing up through the edge of the snow; a few inches from the edge they were in bud, just a few inches further in bloom. Still farther from the snow they had gone to seed. Were there still others under the snow waiting for release? Would they make it before the snows began again?

By the campfire, in this flower-filled world, we thought of other times: of fields of ox-eyed daisies and black-eyed susans we roamed in as children; of deserts in bloom in Arizona, with gaillardias blanketing whole valleys between hazy blue hills; of trails through rainforests strung with orchids.

People have taken flowers to their hearts, though too often exotic, artificially induced blooms in preference to those that grow about us in abundance (have you examined a chickweed lately?). It is disconcerting to realize that flowers evolved not to please us, but as devices for attracting creatures we look upon with disdain (if at all): bees, flies, beetles, and the like. It is even more shattering to consider that flowers are, after all, the sex organs of plants. Meadows of waving genitals, alive with bugs!

Being sedentary, plants cannot copulate with their neighbors, so rely upon insects (or wind, or hummingbirds) to carry their sperm (pollen) to the ovaries of receptive members of their species. But there must be some inducement for the insects, and the flowers provide that inducement by providing sugars in solution (nectar) which feed the insects. Shapes, colors, odors—these serve as lures and guides; and all of the variety we see in a mountain meadow represents a striving for pollination, a search for sexual fulfillment, salvation from the blasts of the coming winter.

The adaptations of flowers for achieving pollination are incredibly diverse and give flowers their individuality. We take these adaptations for granted, as we do so many things. Why is a columbine flower so shaped? To fit the long tongues of hawk moths that are uniquely adapted to penetrate the long spurs for their bounty of nectar and to ensure the set of their seed.

Thomas Eisner and his colleagues at Cornell University have been studying some of the "hidden" qualities of flowers, notably their reflectance of ultraviolet, a color invisible to us but visible to insects. By carrying portable television cameras equipped with ultraviolet transmitting lenses, Dr. Eisner is able to see, on the monitor screen, flowers much as they must appear to their insect visitors. His photographs of marsh marigolds, as seen with the unaided eye and as seen in ultraviolet video, appeared on the cover of *Science* magazine, and remind us of the limitations of our own senses. How much more meaningful the natural world would be if we could now and then explore it with the eye of an insect, the nose of a ferret, or the ear of a bat! But even so, I suspect we would soon find the capacity to take all of this for granted and still take our main gratifications in "thrills" of one kind or another.

I neglected to mention earlier that our discovery of the first pasque flowers of spring was marred by a squadron of trail bikes droning through the valley. Thus we greet the spring: with a roar of motors, crushing the flowers and frightening the birds and mammals. The sentiments evoked by a meadow of flowers are perhaps less titillating than those evoked by a trail bike bumping over stones and splashing through streams. But one's thoughts and feelings can at most pollute a piece of paper, if one is impelled to express them. To wrack a forest with noise, to rut the fields and flatten the flowers, to tint the mountain air with exhaust fumes, to reduce nature to a backdrop for vacuous thrills: if we grant that man was born of nature, it is no less than genocide.

But enough of this. To be granted another spring is the greatest of gifts, and I shall accept it with joy, and with senses honed to the keenest, come what may.

A Meadow in the Rockies
Where the Grass Grows Tall

Not far from our home in the Colorado Rockies there is a bit of landscape that is all too rare: a meadowed valley that is well-watered, ungrazed, unmowed and, for the moment, unthreatened by developers or dam builders.

Grass grows knee-high, and some of the bunchgrass, when in flower, head-high. In the summer there are patches of blue penstemon, pink bergamot and diverse yellow composites, all served by bumblebees and butterflies. Along the stream there are willows as well as dense stands of chokecherries that are visited in late summer by black bears and by local residents eager to begin their yearly round of jelly-making and wine-making.

Visitors in the spring are greeted with the songs of MacGillivray's warblers, song sparrows, black-headed grosbeaks, and, from the hillsides, vesper sparrows and towhees. A pair of red-tailed hawks nest in the pines on the north-facing slope and with harsh calls claim ownership of the valley. Good enough; they will respect its integrity and keep the ground squirrels under control.

We have roamed these meadows so often that they have become a series of places very special to us. A grove of dying aspens is each year visited by a pair of Lewis' woodpeckers, birds of bizarre color and behavior—they often catch insects in the air, as if they were flycatchers. A thicket of hawthorns is the source, each June, of the curious hoots and chuckles of a yellow-breasted chat, another eccentric of the bird world (it is a warbler that doesn't warble).

In one soggy place along the stream we can often flush a snipe, which we suppose could be called a sandpiper gone berserk. Just beyond, in a shady glen, shooting stars spring up from the grass each year. These, too, are eccentrics, primroses that flex their petals upward so that the blossoms seem to be "shooting downward."

In the view of our neighbors, we might be called the most eccentric of the lot, spending so much time watching life in the meadow when we might be fishing or roaring cross-country in an off-road vehicle.

"I had no idea there was so much going on in Heywood's meadow," wrote Henry Thoreau. A meadow is a constant, yet it changes not only seasonally but day by day: flowers coming into bloom or setting seed, birds coming and going, young marmots venturing from the den, a mule deer fawn hidden in the bushes. The valley is in private ownership (not ours); were it federal land it would doubtless be grazed.

Since we are septuagenarians, we are hopeful that we will not see the arrival of "progress" and the departure of the warblers, the marmots, the red-tails and the rest of that radiant society. May we all find meadows as green elsewhere.

18

Canyons

This essay was started some years ago, but rather than finishing it off for publication I have kept it in my files. It is good to have a ragtag essay around, to be added to or lifted from from time to time. It seems a shame to commit it to print and thus render it immutable. But here it is.

I HAVE ALWAYS BEEN HOOKED on canyons. Not necessarily great canyons—the Grand Canyon of the Colorado leaves one searching for words not yet invented. There is much to be said for smaller canyons, which display an intricacy and produce an intimacy that one can take to heart more readily than a mile-deep chasm.

Lately we have been exploring some of the minor canyons that traverse the foothills of the Colorado Rockies. Some are so inconsequential that no one has bothered to name them. Many have only intermittent streams, here persisting as pools sprinkled with water striders, there sinking into the ground to reappear further down, like a dream suddenly remembered. Rocks—massive grays, streaked with black in twisted patterns, eroded in unpredictable ways, chunks of white or rose quartz protruding jaggedly. Rocks—here in sheer cliffs, there in isolated boulders among the sagebrush and mountain mahogany; splashed with lichens in green, orange, gray, or nameless colors. Never the same arrangement of living things upon the nonliving. A rotting stump along a gully; a contorted juniper barely clinging to life; a minuscule waterfall guarded by a squadron of midges; a mourning cloak butterfly leaping from a log.

How quiet the canyon: the wind in the trees, the call of a jay, a faint tinkling in the streambed. Yet the canyon would not be here if the tinkling were the stream's only voice. On a summer evening, after a thunderstorm, great torrents must rush down the canyon, rolling boulders, tearing out trees, deepening the gash in the mountains by a millimeter or two. Out of an orgy of torrent and rock, in time, a harebell springs from a mossy bank.

The memory of canyons sticks to one like cockleburs. I remember Canyon de Lobos, in Mexico, where a great cloud of butterflies greeted me; Madera Canyon, in Arizona, a shady sanctuary after a scorching day in the desert; Sitting Bull Canyon in New Mexico, blocked by a great mass of tufa over which the stream tumbled in a thousand showers of droplets, to be reunited in quiet pools below; the Black Canyon of the Gunnison, in Colorado— as if some deific but nervous surgeon had sliced the earth's skin and revealed its black soul.

I remember a nameless canyon in the Everard Ranges of central Australia. In recesses in the walls the aborigines had left records of their thoughts and emotions: abstract, tortuous patterns in black, white, and red. Symbols of spirits of the Dreamtime, one supposes, and a great multicolored snake, the rainbow serpent that brings rain all too seldom to these parched lands. This canyon may well have been sacred to the aborigines; at the very least they must have appreciated the tall gum trees and the massive heaps of granite hiding bright-eyed rock wallabies. Huddled close to their fires by night, hunting and gathering plants by day—who can say their lives were inferior to ours? They maintained an intimate and enduring working relationship with the earth that our brittle modern world may someday envy.

It was in a renowned canyon, Olduvai Gorge, that Louis Leakey found evidence of a very much more ancient race of humans.

Olduvai Gorge is a remote place in the northern part of Tanzania, not notable for its natural beauty, but teeming with the bones of extinct creatures. I heard Louis Leakey lecture a few years before he died—a great bear of a man who had struggled with insufficient funds, with rocks that yielded secrets only after years of grueling work, and with skeptical anthropologists.

In Canyonlands, Utah, we found images painted on canyon walls, recognizable hunters and their kill. Here and there we found bits of chipped jasper, remains of their weapons, and deep in the canyons remains of their homes built into cavities in the walls. The Indians of the Southwest still exist, of course, as do the Australian aborigines, and some still retain a measure of their dignity and their ancestral ways. But western culture has been an irresistible force, and those that survived smallpox and tuberculosis have mainly succumbed to creeping "progress" and often to its major antidote, alcohol.

Nowhere can one feel so great a respect for the history of the earth as in Utah's Canyonlands. Here canyons are the norm, the spaces between them sometimes no more than ridges or pinnacles of reddish sandstone crowned with resistant white caprock. How many thousands of years it must have taken to lay down such great thicknesses of sandstone, and how many more tens of thousands, in a land of so little rain, to carve them into such a labyrinth.

Our last trip to Canyonlands was in March, when it was still cool enough to climb about with pleasure. A few wildflowers were already in bloom, and the canyon wrens were in full song—a burst of notes descending the scale, like the history of the canyons themselves, down, down, down. How wrong if the canyon wren's song ascended the scale! And how different it might sound somewhere else, without the canyon walls to provide a resonating chamber for so small a bird.

"I cannot conceive of a more worthless and impracticable region than the one we now find ourselves in." So wrote Captain

John Macomb, one of the early explorers of Canyonlands, in 1859. True, it is not a place to plant soybeans or start a pizza parlor. Thank God for worthless places, places immune to human "development." These canyons are much as the Indians must have found them when they first entered the area, and the rock walls document times when man was still an improbable product of earth history.

To be sure, canyons can at times be hazardous to people and to the plants and animals living there. I well remember a trip down a narrow, winding track into the canyon of the Canadian River, in northern New Mexico. Camped by the river, we were subjected to one very wet thunderstorm after another. We spent the night worrying whether the river would rise to the level of our tent. It did not rise quite that high, but we had real doubts that the road out would be passable. It was, barely. Backpacking along the Gila River in southern New Mexico, we stopped to rest in a light rain beside a seemingly innocuous side-canyon that suddenly became an angry torrent. We were above the flood, but had left our backpacks on the opposite side of the stream, and had no choice but to wait for the stream to subside. Of course neither of these experiences was at all comparable to massive flash floods such as the one that scoured out Big Thompson Canyon, in Colorado, in 1976, killing 145 people. Streams are, after all, the builders of canyons, and it is in their character to display their power occasionally.

One can go back in time almost anywhere there is a canyon. Colorado's Front Range will do very well. One might start in the narrows of this same Big Thompson Canyon, a major tourist route into Rocky Mountain National Park. Here one is in the heart of masses of Precambrian schists and granites, formed when the seas were empty of any but the most tentative of organisms. Proceeding eastward to the mouth of the canyon, one is suddenly in a very different world: the rocks are stratified, and tilted steeply toward the mountains. These are sedimentary rocks of a much later era that were bent upward when the Rockies were formed, then eroded by streams emerging from the uplifted mountains. Some are resistant sandstones that form the crests of parallel rows of hogbacks, others more easily eroded shales and sandstones that form the slopes and valleys between, now mostly covered with grasses. Going east from the canyon mouth, successive hogbacks are of progressively more recently formed rocks, passing all the way from Pennsylvanian to Cretaceous strata—a span of over 150 million years in time. The most easterly of these is the "Devil's Backbone," a long, ragged crest of resistant but decaying sandstone formed some 130 million years ago. We climbed the Devil's Backbone one winter day, crawling over jumbles of rock, squeezing through crevices, frightening a swirl of pigeons that have adopted it as home, consorting with the ghosts of dinosaurs.

Indeed, it is from the so-called Morrison formation, which forms part of the slope of this easternmost hogback, that evidence of some of the largest of dinosaurs has come. In his book *The Bone Hunters*, Url Lanham tells how Arthur Lake, a school teacher in Golden, Colorado, turned up a huge bone in the Morrison formation in 1877 and sent it to Professor O. C. Marsh at Yale University. Marsh opined that the dinosaur Lake had discovered must have been at least fifty feet long. Since then even larger ones have been found—"superdinosaurs," in Lanham's words.

Canyons dissect the earth like zoologists dissecting earthworms, revealing things one would never have suspected were there. Eons of time we really cannot grasp; movements of seas, heaving of mountains, soughing of the wind through forests that now power our automobiles. In the mad pace of our lives, it is good now and then to stop and fondle a chunk of Jurassic sandstone, to scratch with reverence a cliff of Precambrian schist, to project oneself momentarily into prehuman epochs when the pace was slow, the goal a small piece of the world in which to dream and to die, and to leave a bit of oneself to dream and die again. Loren Eiseley put it well in *The Firmament of Time*:

"It is with the coming of man that a vast hole seems to open in nature, a vast black whirlpool spinning faster and faster, consuming flesh, stones, soil, minerals, sucking down the lightning, wrenching power from the atom, until the ancient sounds of nature are drowned in the cacophony of something which is no longer nature, something instead which is loose and knocking at the world's heart. ..."

19

A Pile of Rocks

Age brings reduced mobility, and a closer focus on one's immediate surroundings.
Orion *published this essay in their spring issue, 1991. References to the Long*
Expedition reflect the fact that I was at the time working on my book The Natural
History of the Long Expedition to the Rocky Mountains, 1819–1820, *
published by the Oxford University Press in 1995.*

WHEN WE DECIDED TO BUILD our house in the Rocky
Mountains beside a great, jumbled pile of granite boulders, we
willingly sacrificed the opportunity to have the well-groomed
lawn that has become part of the formula for "gracious living."
And we soon discovered that the denizens of our rock pile—marmots, chipmunks, rabbits, pack rats, and golden-mantled ground
squirrels—made gardening impossible. All can live nicely on a
diet of succulent plants that grow among the rocks or in nearby
meadows, but for some reason anything *we* plant seems to them
especially desirable. So we have settled into a peaceful coexistence, and simply enjoy all these handsome critters.

In winter, most animals are sleeping deep in hidden places, but
the rocks are alive with snow drifting in curious patterns among
the boulders. And the lichens are always there, splotching the
rocks with pastel greens, yellows, and browns. A few small weather-
beaten pines and junipers are green through the winter, providing stopping-off places for mountain chickadees and Steller's jays

on the way to our feeders. Now and then a tassel-eared squirrel
perches on the snow-covered rocks, also eying our feeders: a
study of black on white. But it is in the spring that the real drama
begins. Grasses spring up between the boulders, yellow ragworts
and blue penstemons bloom where there is soil enough, and the
bushes leaf out—squaw currants, thimbleberries, and waxflowers.
Soon they will blossom, attracting bumblebees and butterflies.
Marmots sun themselves, and chipmunks and ground squirrels
dash about as if they had only a few months in the sun (as of
course they do).

One day the rock wren will be back, performing regularly from
the topmost rocks. We speak of him as "our" rock wren, though
we have no way of knowing whether it is the male that performed
there last year, his son, or a male from elsewhere that has occupied a territory left vacant when another failed to return. In any
case the song is similar, in fact all four or five songs, delivered in
an unpredictable pattern. How does he decide which to sing at a
particular moment? Does each convey a different message, or a
different facet of his volatile spirit? Now it is *chewee, chewee, chewee*;
now *ple, ple, ple, ple*; now *tipi, tipi, tipi, tipi*; now *br-r-r-r-r*. A song
not perhaps as evocative of the wilds as that of the canyon wren,
as insistent as that of the cactus wren, or as homey as that of the
house wren, but more varied and ear-catching than any of those.

Thomas Say was evidently not greatly impressed with rock
wrens when he discovered them near the mouth of South Platte
Canyon (southwest of what is now Denver) in 1820. He called
the species the obscure wren and gave it the scientific name
Troglodytes obsoleta. He had little to say about it aside from the
coloration of its plumage, which he found to be "of a much more
sombre hue" than that of the Carolina wren of the East. Say was
trudging along the foothills of the Rockies as a member of the
Long Expedition, committed to covering many miles a day by
foot and horseback as he collected specimens of animals and
plants new or little known to science. If Say and his companions

reveled in the scenery or the birds and wildflowers, it is not apparent from their narrative, which more often tells of fatigue, hunger, and illness.

All through June the wrens perform, and by now the waxflowers are blooming from nearly every crevice, another reminder of the Long Expedition. Edwin James, the expedition's botanist and physician, collected the first waxflowers known to science a few days before or after he made the first ascent of Pikes Peak and studied its alpine flora. His specimens eventually found their way to John Torrey and Asa Gray, the leading botanists of the day. Torrey and Gray named the plant *Jamesia americana*, "in commemoration of the scientific services of its discoverer [who] made an excellent collection of plants under the most unfavorable circumstances."

It is hard to believe that there is enough soil in crevices among the rocks to provide sustenance for this handsome shrub with its faintly fragrant, waxy white blossoms. *Jamesia* is a unique plant, the only member of the hydrangea family in the West and a plant with a long geological pedigree. Fossils of the genus have been found in rocks near Creede, Colorado, dating from 35 million years ago. Perhaps the shrubs have survived by clinging to a habitat where there is little competition from other plants.

We can count on the waxflowers blooming each June, and so far the rock wren has come back each year. Every summer the ground squirrels, chipmunks, and other herbivores are active. Now and then a predator appears: a long-tailed weasel slithering among the rocks, a pigmy owl perched in a pine, a golden eagle pausing briefly to survey the area from a promontory. We think of these rocks as our private wilderness area. Now that federally designated wilderness areas are under siege for "locking up" lands that might be used for economic benefit, and the Endangered Species Act is threatened with dilution to save jobs for loggers, it is surely appropriate for landowners to take matters into their own hands to the extent they are able. Admittedly there is not sufficient habitat here for elk or bears, and we have so far waited in vain for a cougar to stop by on his prowls. But if enough neighbors resolve to live with nature rather than against it, there may be hope even for these.

What will become of these rocks when we are gone we do not know. It is hard to believe that this heap of boulders is valuable enough to disturb. Then again "moss rocks" (that is, lichen-covered rocks) have become popular for building and for lawn decorations, and outcrops not far away are being dismantled for profit.

For now, though, our rock pile is pristine enough to remind us of men who traveled this way nearly two centuries ago. Admittedly we exploit it in our own way, as the plants and animals entertain us endlessly. Indeed we need them desperately, as a counter to our darker thoughts: of a planet grossly overpopulated by our kind, motivated by ethics that are wholly human-oriented.

Only a pile of rocks, but a microcosm of the planet as it might be, with humans as participants rather than destroyers.

20

A Stick of Wood

This piece was rejected by three journals, but I still like it, perhaps because I have spent so many hours in recent years with axe in hand. It was wood for warmth that permitted early man to migrate from Africa into the "temperate" zones. Perhaps there is a bit of the primitive in me. I hope so.

A SWING OF THE AXE, and the sharp crack of split wood. A satisfying sound. Inside our cabin, the wood will keep us warm and will sputter softly while the winds scream outside. I have long since discovered that there is little I can do to steer humanity toward saner courses, but I can split a log. It is a grand release, a goal quickly achieved, a brief moment of success in a life of striving for the unattainable.

And there are stories in the wood. This log is riddled with the burrows of beetle larvae, forming surrealistic patterns deep in the heartwood. Here is such a larva, a bundle of flesh still soft and very much alive in midwinter. Left alone, it would have produced an elegant longhorned beetle next summer. Having destroyed its home, I remove it to my bird feeder, where it is quickly harvested by a jay.

As I split, the bark peels off, revealing the complex tracing of bark beetles, which are known to carry the spores of a fungus that is often fatal to these ponderosa pines. The beetles are hardly larger than a grain of rice, but they attack the trees *en masse*. Pine

195

trees are not without their defenses. An invading bark beetle is quickly smothered in pitch, and only by invading by the hundreds can the beetles overcome the tree's resistance. When the tree's defenses are exhausted, other beetles can bore deeply into the trunk, leaving passageways for fungi. When the last of its needles have fallen, the tree is left gaunt and naked, silently waiting for a wind that will send it crashing to the ground. Very likely it was the beetles and the fungi they carry that killed this tree. In any case the tree was ripe for harvesting for firewood, the wood already seasoned but not yet subject to rot, the tree not too big for me to handle with axe and handsaw, but big enough to provide plenty of splitable wood.

This was not a venerable tree, about ninety years old, if I read the growth rings correctly. So it was born about the turn of the century, a time when humans were less common hereabouts than the mule deer that still roam these hills. The few roads were little more than wagon tracks, the houses widely spaced, where families read by kerosene lamp and cooked simple meals over a wood-fed iron range. How times have changed, and how we have grown apart from nature! Perhaps that is another reason why I so enjoy woodsplitting; I delude myself that I live in a time when nature mattered, a time when I can reach out to nature to fill my modest needs.

Perhaps the pine was born in soil thrown up by a pocket gopher, since the gophers are plentiful here, and pine seedlings do not thrive in competition with grasses and wildflowers. For a few years it probably grew slowly in the shade of other trees, then began to shoot up as its neighbors died or fell to a woodsman's axe. Here on the eastern slopes of the Rockies, pines rarely grow large enough to be useful for building timbers, but they are good for log cabins, mine props, railroad ties, and of course for firewood. Only in ravines, or on well-watered slopes farther west, do ponderosas become truly "ponderous."

In forty or fifty years the tree reached sexual maturity and began to produce clouds of pollen and tough, seed-bearing cones.

How many of the trillions of pollen grains produced through the years found their way to female strobili? How many seeds produced new trees? Are any of the nearby small trees offspring of this pine? Surely no more than a very few. Small pines are often browsed or trampled by deer, or by the cattle that for a time spent their summers here.

Yet this tree survived, stood boldly through storms, and was spared the lightning that shredded other trees on this hill. The United States Forest Service lists nearly two hundred kinds of insects that attack ponderosa pines, but this tree lived for many years before succumbing to one or more of them. While it lived, it was a stopping place for Steller's jays and pine siskins, in summer for wood pewees and western tanagers. Its seeds were harvested by tassel-eared squirrels, chipmunks, and blue grouse. Deer slept in its shade, and perhaps a black bear lumbered by and stopped to sharpen its claws. Ravens called from the top, and for a time a great horned owl roosted among the branches. When it began to weaken and die, hairy woodpeckers and white-breasted nuthatches scouted the trunk and branches for insects. Had it been left to fall, it would have made a home for deer mice, and eventually its remains would crumble and enrich the soil. While alive it grasped the sunlight and made it into greenery and wood. It was a good and useful life, terminated too soon. But it will keep us warm this winter, and as smoke from the chimney rise heavenward more surely than ever will I.

We take trees for granted, as we do so much of nature. They do not speak to us except as they sough in the wind. "Of all pines," wrote John Muir of the ponderosa, "this one gives forth the finest music to the winds." There is a reason for this: the needles are long, the trees and their branches spaced such that the wind seeks them out, playing on them as if on a giant, rustic harp. Trees consume nothing but sunshine, rain, and a few soil nutrients. Every tree is a gift of beauty, of shade and shelter, of oxygen, potentially of wood, even of chemicals (such as taxol) that may prove useful to us.

Do trees have a conscience, are they aware of the winds, of the birds that nest in their branches? Surely not, as we understand such matters. Yet they have a right to a piece of the planet, as do all living things. They live lives on their own terms, incidentally enriching the planet in many ways. As givers (as opposed to takers, that is, animals and people) they surely have special rights and special claims on our respect. Where trees are few, as in a city, a suburban yard, or outside a study window, it is easy to develop an affection for individual trees. In a forest it is more difficult, but there should be no lessening of respect for individual trees. Each is no less a giver.

I shall need to split many logs to survive this winter, but each split will be as welcome as the last. Spring breezes will one day waken nature, and the axe will be put to rest until, with luck, I shall pick it up again in the fall.

Index

abamectin, 162
Academy of Natural Sciences of
   Philadelphia, 135
Aculeate wasps, 77
adenosine triphosphate (ATP), 59–60, 61
Agassiz, Alexander, 26
Agassiz, Louis, 22–23, 24–25, 31, 32, 35
Agassiz Museum, 26, 33
agriculture
   Green Revolution, 155
   pest problems and pesticide use,
     155–59, 164–65
   potential value of taxonomic
     research, 77
   See also pest control
Akeley, Carl, 27–30
Alaska, Bering expedition, 169
albatross, 149
Aldrovandi, Ulysses, 58
Alexander, R. D., 79–80
Alexander, Richard, 41
Allis, Edward P., Jr., 30
altruism, 108–10
American cockroach, 44–45, 47–48,
   49, 51
American Entomologist, 96
American Fur Company, 175
American Museum of Natural History,
   28–29, 32
American Ornithology, 173
Anderson, John, 24
*Ants: Their Structure, Development, and
   Behavior* (Wheeler), 102
ants, 19, 33, 101–2
   altruism and kin selection, 108, 109
   fire ants, 104–5, 162
   odor trails, 104–5

The Ants (Wilson and Hölldobler),
   116
The Ants of Switzerland (Forel), 102
aphid, Russian wheat, 156–57
Aporus, 78
archy and mehitabel (Marquis), 43
Aristotle, 58
armyworms, 94
arsenical chemicals, 97
Artedi, Peter, 71
asparagus beetles, 91–92
Astragalus purshii, 175
ATP, 59–60, 61
audio mimicry, 40
Audubon, John James, 174, 176, 177
Australia
   canyon pictographs, 186
   insect fauna, 78
   invasive cacti, 76
Australian birds, 8, 9, 133–51
   Australian magpies, 135–36
   bee-eaters, 145
   black swan, 137
   bower birds, 138–40
   butcher birds, 136
   climate adaptations, 148
   currawongs, 136–37
   early study of, 134–35
   emu, 140–41, 148
   honeyeaters, 137, 143–45
   kookaburras, 8, 134, 146–47
   lyrebirds, 9, 136, 137–38, 140
   mound-builders, 140, 141–43
   mudlark, 137
   other species of interest, 150–51
   parrots and relatives, 134, 143, 148
   social behavior, 144–47, 148